D1126047

PRACTICAL
SHOWJUMPING

WARD LOCK RIDING SCHOOL

Know Your Pony
Understanding Your Horse
Learning to Ride
Discovering Dressage
Tack and Clothing
Understanding Fitness and Training
Eventing
Modern Stable Management

PRACTICAL
SHOWJUMPING

JUDITH DRAPER

WARD LOCK

RIDING SCHOOL

WARD LOCK

A WARD LOCK BOOK

First published in the UK 1993
by Ward Lock
Villiers House
41/47 Strand
LONDON WC2N 5JE

A Cassell Imprint

Text © Judith Draper 1993

All rights reserved. No part of this book may be
reproduced or transmitted in any form or by any
means, electronic or mechanical, including photo-
copying, recording or any information storage and
retrieval system, without prior permission in writing from the copyright holder and Publisher.

Distributed in the United States by Sterling
Publishing Co., Inc., 387 Park Avenue South, New
York, NY 10016-8810

Distributed in Australia by Capricorn Link
(Australia) Pty Ltd, P.O. Box 665, Lane Cove,
NSW 2066

A British Library Cataloguing in Publication Data
block for this book may be obtained from the
British Library

ISBN 0 7063 7135 6

Printed and bound in Great Britain by
Hillman Printers (Frome) Ltd

All photographs by Kit Houghton

*Frontispiece: In your first competition it is always
important to look straight ahead to the next fence.*

CONTENTS

THE AUTHOR

Judith Draper is a freelance equestrian writer who has been involved with horses all her life. Practical involvement included several seasons in flat and National Hunt stables before she turned to journalism. She spent 13 years on the editorial staff of the monthly magazine *Riding*, was equestrian correspondent of *The Daily Mail* from 1988-91 and currently writes regularly for *The Mail on Sunday*.

She is editor of the British Horse Society's magazine *British Horse* and a regular contributor to equestrian magazines throughout the world. Previous books include *Milton, Super Champion, Teach Yourself Show Jumping, The Stars of Show Jumping* and the sport's definitive book of results and records, published by Guinness, *Show Jumping: Records, Facts and Champions*.

INTRODUCTION

Show jumping is one of the most popular equestrian sports in the world. Today, leading riders from dozens of different countries compete at international level, while many more, less-ambitious horse lovers enjoy taking part in competitions at national or local shows.

The sport's great popularity is easy to understand as most people who have grasped the basics of horsemanship get a tremendous thrill from riding over fences, however small. Also, because jumping takes place in a relatively small area, over brightly coloured obstacles, and has easy-to-follow rules, it is attractive to spectators. Perhaps show jumping's biggest advantage over most non-horse sports is that men and women or boys and girls can compete against each other on equal terms.

Surprisingly, jumping on horseback is a relatively new pastime. Although humans have been riding horses for thousands of years, jumping seems only to have become common during the last few centuries. The sport of show jumping can trace its roots to the need for horses to negotiate an increasing number of man-made obstacles, such as hedges and fences, when

going across country. As hunting and racing began to grow in popularity, so jumping turned into a sport. However, jumping over fences in an arena was not seen until towards the end of the nineteenth century and to begin with the obstacles merely resembled those seen out hunting. As an international sport, jumping was confined mainly to cavalry officers until the Second World War.

Although women were allowed to compete quite early on, they were often restricted to their own classes and it was not until some years after the war that they were allowed to ride in official teams. By that time most countries' armies had become totally mechanized and the sport had to be opened up to civilians if it was to survive.

Nowadays everyone can take part and whether you are a complete novice or an experienced rider, have a 12.2 h.h. pony or a 17 h.h. Thoroughbred, you will have no difficulty in finding competitions to suit you. In Britain, where the governing body is the British Show Jumping Association, there is a range of classes, from novice to national championship level, for both junior members (not over the age of sixteen) and adults, with some special classes, too, for young riders (not over twenty-one), who are also eligible to compete (on horses) against their seniors. Juniors may ride ponies of varying sizes up to 14.2 h.h. (148 cm), depending on their age group.

Ponies and horses are graded according to the amount of prize money they have won. The rules concerning the size of fences that they are asked to jump in each grade are very strict so that there is no risk of a talented youngster being overfaced. Novice horses are registered as Grade C and may begin their jumping careers in special Novice competitions, before progressing to Newcomers and

Foxhunter. When they have earned enough prize money, they move up into Grade B and eventually into the top grade, A.

In the United States, where the governing body is the American Horse Shows Association, horses are again graded according to prize money won and may compete in Preliminary, Intermediate, Open and Amateur Owner Jumper classes. There are also competitions for juniors up to the age of eighteen. In addition, America has a very useful equitation division, which includes jumping classes. These are judged on the performance of the rider only and provide marvellous experience for the novice wanting to perfect his or her technique.

CHAPTER 1

CHOOSING THE RIGHT HORSE FOR JUMPING

Before you set out to learn to show jump, at whatever standard, it is important to bear in mind that jumping is not a natural activity for horses and ponies. You have only to study the way they are made – long legs, large lungs, large heart – to realize that they are designed for galloping, which, in the wild, would help them to escape from predators. Given the choice, a horse or pony will almost always go round, not over, any obstruction that he finds in his way. It is not particularly difficult to train them to jump, however, and most appear to enjoy it once they have been shown what to do, although that is definitely a job for an experienced trainer, not a novice rider.

How successful a horse becomes as a show jumper depends on a number of factors. Most horses will progress to jumping fences up to about 1.22 m (4 ft) quite success-fully but many go no further, either because they lack the necessary physical ability or they find jump-ing round after round of coloured fences boring. Some are simply not careful enough. Interestingly, many horses that have reached their limit in show jumping go on to become successful three-day event horses,

where the solid fences are never higher than 1.2 m (3 ft 11 in).

HOW THE HORSE JUMPS

Just as it is important for the novice rider to learn to walk, trot and canter on a horse that has been correctly schooled, so it is vital for someone learning to jump to do so on a horse that has been given a good grounding in the basics of jumping and understands what is required of him. It also helps the rider to understand why they need to sit in jumping position and fold over the jumps if they also under-stand how the horse jumps.

As a horse approaches a fence, he gathers himself together ready to spring off the ground, taking a slightly shorter last stride. The front part of the horse (the fore-hand), made up of the head, neck, withers, shoulders and front legs, is his heaviest part and in order to raise his forehand off the ground, the horse has to shift his weight back over his hind legs.

Just before he takes off, he stretches out his neck and lowers his head a little as he sizes up the obstacle and judges his take-off.

Approach   Take-off   Flight

Then, as he takes off, he raises his head and neck and thrusts himself upwards and forwards. A good show jumper also quickly folds up his forelegs to avoid hitting the fence 'in front'.

As the horse reaches the highest point of a jump, his head and neck begin to lower and his hindquarters rise level with his forehand. If the horse is a good jumper, he lifts his hind legs at the stifle and stretches out his legs in order to avoid hitting the fence 'behind'.

His forelegs touch down first, followed by his hind legs and then he gathers himself together ready for the first canter stride to the next fence.

The rounder the horse's outline is over a fence, the easier it is for him to clear it with the least effort. A horse that jumps with his head in the air and his back flat has to go higher in order to clear the same height. This wastes energy and often leads to mistakes.

It is the rider's job to interfere with the horse as little as possible once he starts his jump, by sitting still and staying in balance with the horse at all stages of the jump – the take-off, the flight and the landing.

HOW THE HORSE LEARNS TO JUMP

A horse is taught to jump by first being walked, then trotted, over a pole on the ground. Once he will go back and forth over this with confidence, the trainer places a second pole on the ground parallel to the first. The distance between the two poles is carefully adjusted to suit the individual horse's stride. At this stage everything is made as easy as possible for him so that he does not trip over the poles and frighten or injure himself. Gradually more poles are added, one at a time, until the horse is trotting happily down a line of six poles.

Trotting poles are the basis of all jumping training. They make the horse more supple and improve his balance because, to go over them, he has to lower his head and neck

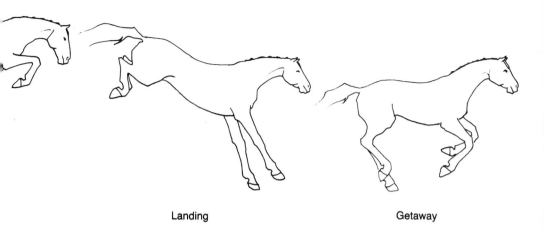

Landing

Getaway

How the horse jumps.

and round his back. They encourage him to lift his legs higher than when doing work on the flat and also help him to improve the co-ordination of the movement of his legs.

Most trainers introduce trotting poles into a horse's training quite early on. Work over poles makes a change from flatwork and helps to keep the horse interested in his schooling. He can either be ridden over them or worked over them on the lunge, in which case the poles

The first jumping lesson: walking over a pole on the ground.

The first jump: a cross-pole fence encourages the pony to jump straight and over the centre of the obstacle. The placing pole puts him in the correct spot for take-off.

Left: *A horse with good overall conformation for jumping.*
Right: *Poor confirmation, unsuitable for jumping.*

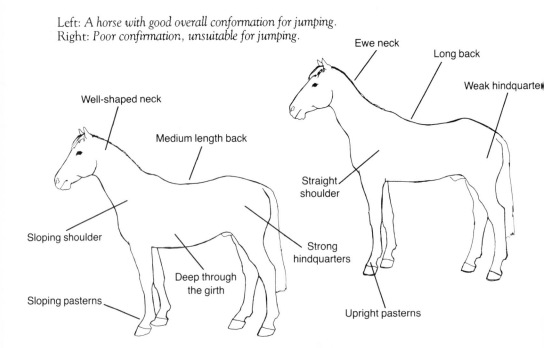

Ewe neck

Long back

Weak hindquarter

Well-shaped neck

Medium length back

Straight shoulder

Sloping shoulder

Strong hindquarters

Deep through the girth

Upright pasterns

Sloping pasterns

Conformation in the Show Jumper
What to Look For, What to Avoid

Neck

A medium-length, slightly arched neck makes it easier for the horse to jump with a rounded outline.

A short 'upside down' neck (ewe neck) tends to give the horse a high head carriage, which means he will have to jump higher than really necessary to clear a fence with his hindquarters.

Shoulders

Sloping shoulders enable the horse to lengthen his stride easily – essential in show jumping, especially when jumping doubles and trebles – and also give the rider a comfortable ride.

Upright shoulders tend to produce a jarring action and short strides. They also put a lot of strain on the horse's legs as he lands over fences.

Body

A medium-length back, with good depth through the girth, indicates strength. A deep rib cage gives the horse's internal organs plenty of room to function correctly – important for horses who are asked to do strenuous work like jumping.

A very long back usually denotes weakness.

Legs

Short cannon bones, fairly large knees and hocks and flattish, rather than rounded, fetlock joints indicate strength. In a horse of around 16 h.h. the circumference of the cannon bone beneath the knee should measure at least 20 cm (8 in). Viewed from the side the legs should appear to drop down vertically from the horse, not slope backwards or forwards.

Puffiness around the tendons at the back of the legs, or in the joints, indicates strain or injury. Very long pasterns (between the fetlock joints and the feet) are prone to weakness; short upright ones cause the horse to jar his legs when he jumps. The hind legs will be weak if the hocks are high off the ground or turn inwards or outwards.

Feet

The strongest feet are those that are rounded in appearance and look like matching pairs. Strong feet are essential in the show jumper. When the horse lands over a fence, he puts one forefoot down slightly in advance of the other, putting his entire enormous weight (not to mention yours) on that one hoof.

Small, narrow feet do not give sufficient shock absorption. Those that turn in or out are liable to be weak and may cause a horse to knock himself when he jumps.

are set on a curve. Working the young horse on the lunge without a rider can be very beneficial as it puts less strain on his back and limbs.

The horse's first actual jump is over a very low cross-pole, no more than about 38 cm (15 in) high, placed after the line of trotting poles at a distance of about 2.7 m (9 ft) from the final pole. This enables the horse to land over the last pole and jump the little fence without having to take a stride between the two. Again the distance is adjusted to suit the individual horse.

The reason for using a cross-pole fence instead of an ordinary, straight rail is to direct the horse to the centre of the obstacle. Getting the horse to jump straight and in the centre of his fences from the start helps him to develop a good jumping style.

HOW THE RIDER LEARNS TO JUMP

Just as trotting poles form the basis of all jumping training for the horse, so they are also used to introduce the rider to the art of riding over fences. Trotting a correctly trained horse over poles on the ground forms the rider's first jumping lesson. Work over trotting poles improves the novice rider's balance, co-ordination and security in the saddle in preparation for actual jumping.

Similarly, a cross-pole fence makes an ideal start for the rider because if you make the jump as easy as possible for the horse, the rider can concentrate on his or her own position in the saddle instead of worrying about whether the horse will actually jump the fence.

For a complete beginner to try to master the jumping seat on an animal who doesn't understand what is wanted of him is quite clearly asking for trouble, which is why, when buying a horse for jumping, it is so important to make absolutely sure that he has received a good basic grounding over fences.

CHOOSING A HORSE FOR SHOW JUMPING

Good show jumping horses come in all shapes and sizes. Often it is a case of the right temperament and general attitude to jumping being more important than absolutely correct conformation. Certainly, many of the horses (and for that matter ponies) who do well in the jumping ring would never win a rosette in a show class!

The most successful are those born with natural athletic ability – something that usually becomes obvious as soon as they have their first lessons over small obstacles – and the courage and keenness to take on a challenge.

However, the way a horse is put together – his conformation – is still of great importance because of the considerable strain put on a horse's body and limbs when he jumps. It is far easier to train a well-proportioned horse to jump with

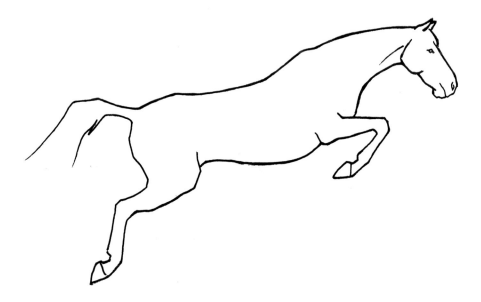

A horse showing good technique over a jump: a rounded outline and front legs folded up.

A horse showing poor technique over a jump: dangling forelegs, flat back and trailing back legs.

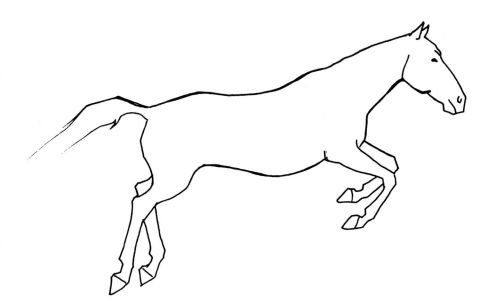

the minimum of effort than one who has physical defects, while he is much less liable to suffer injuries if he is basically a strong type of animal.

In all horses the 'engine' is at the back and in the show jumper, in particular, the hindquarters should be broad and round and give an impression of strength and power. This is where the horse gets his spring from and horses with weak-looking quarters rarely make good jumpers.

Suiting the horse to the rider is important in all aspects of equestrian sport but particularly so in jumping where it is so easy for a bad experience to put a rider off for life. A timid rider will have no fun on a strong, excitable horse; a brave, positive rider will soon grow tired of a lazy horse. Generally speaking, there isn't any point, either, in a small rider buying a huge horse or a tall person buying a small one. It is much easier to ride well on a horse who suits you physically as well as in temperament.

When you go to look at a horse you are thinking of buying, it is always a good idea to take along a more experienced person who can advise you on the animal's suitability for your needs and your riding ability. The owner will put the horse through his paces while you watch and then you can have a ride to see whether you like the horse. However, if you are not yet ready to jump him yourself, it is advisable to ask another person – perhaps your riding instructor – to have a ride on him and give you an independent opinion about his level of training, his temperament and his suitability for you.

It is all too easy for an experienced rider, who is used to a particular horse, to make him look absolutely wonderful during a short demonstration ride, only for you to find, when you get the horse home, that he is not quite as well trained as he looked. If your independent assistant is a good rider and has also seen what *you* can do on a horse, he or she will be able to advise on whether this is the one for you.

Watching a horse jump on the lunge or loose in a school is another good way of assessing his jumping technique, although this is not always possible to arrange.

CHAPTER 2

EQUIPMENT FOR THE HORSE AND RIDER

You don't need a vast amount of expensive, sophisticated equipment to learn to show jump but what you do use must comply with sensible safety precautions.

The costliest item is, of course, the horse himself and then comes a good jumping saddle. A variety of practice fences is essential and you will need to set aside a flat area of ground to use for schooling. Good ready-made fences can be bought from specialist manufacturers, but if cash is short it is not that difficult to construct your own if you use your imagination and have a relative or friend who is good at DIY!

For shows, you will need the correct clothes for yourself. These will depend, to a certain extent, on the level at which you are competing.

THE JUMPING SADDLE

The modern jumping saddle is specially designed to help the rider to stay in balance with the horse through all the different phases of jumping. Balance, in fact, is the key word in jumping. The rider must be in perfect balance with the horse, not only over the fences but also on the flat between obstacles if the

horse is to show jump successfully, with minimum interference from the weight on his back.

Many people use a general purpose saddle when they start to jump. Although it is perfectly possible to adopt a good forward seat in such a saddle, most riders find it easier to do so in one designed specially for the job, especially when they start to jump bigger fences.

The tree (the basic framework) on which a jumping saddle is made differs from that used for a general purpose saddle in that the attachments from which the stirrup leathers hang (the bars) are placed further forward. Because the rider needs to have shorter stirrups for jumping than when riding on the flat, the leg is carried in a different position. Jumping with short stirrups in a general purpose saddle can cause the rider's lower leg to swing back because the bars are not far enough forward. Backward movement of the lower leg affects the rider's balance and, in turn, that of the horse.

On a jumping saddle tree, the stirrup leathers hang down vertically when you are in the forward seat and so enable you to keep your lower leg in the correct position.

As with all riding, it is essential for the saddle to fit both the horse and the rider. Be wary of buying a horse together with its tack. If you are a different size and shape from the previous owner, the chances are that the saddle will not fit *you*.

Always use a good quality numnah under your saddle to provide extra cushioning for the horse's back but don't fall into the trap of thinking that a numnah will make up for a badly fitting saddle – it won't. Strong girths are essential for jumping and it is a good idea to fit a surcingle over the top of the saddle as well, to give additional security.

Use good quality stirrup leathers and strong stainless steel irons. If your horse has high withers, fit a breastgirth or breastplate. In fact, it is a good idea always to use one regardless of your horse's conformation just in case your saddle slips for another reason, such as a loose girth.

BRIDLES AND BITS

There are no hard and fast rules about which bridle and bit you should use in show jumping. The higher up the sport you go, the more complicated bitting arrange-

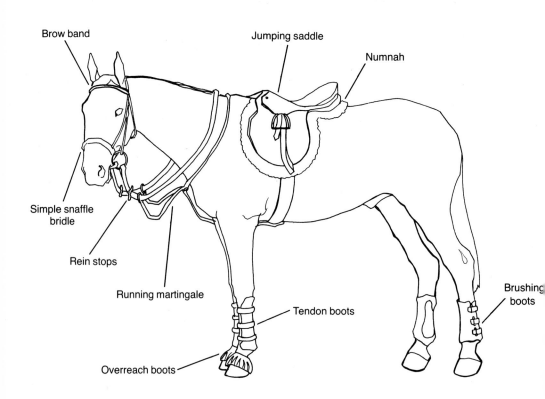

Brow band
Jumping saddle
Numnah
Simple snaffle bridle
Rein stops
Running martingale
Tendon boots
Brushing boots
Overreach boots

The horse dressed to go jumping.

ments you will tend to see, but these are definitely for experts only. An enormous amount of damage can be done to a horse's mouth (and his confidence) by severe gadgets employed by the wrong hands.

As a general rule, the simpler the bridle the better. If a horse has been well schooled from the beginning, he should go perfectly well in a snaffle bridle with a cavesson noseband. Of course, some horses are stronger than others and you may need to change to a slightly stronger bit as your horse becomes fitter. Much will depend on his character and your riding ability.

Some horses are happier with a straight bar bit rather than a jointed one. Often the deciding factor is the shape of the horse's mouth. If you have trouble in deciding what suits your particular horse, it is best to get advice from an expert. Whatever bridle your horse wears, it must fit perfectly, and so must the bit. A horse who is uncomfortable in his head, perhaps because his browband is pinching his ears or his throatlash is too tight, or in his mouth because the bit is too big or too small or fitted too high or too low, will never make a good show jumper.

Remember that you may find yourself competing in wet weather so be sure to choose reins that give you good grip, such as rubber-covered ones.

Although, on the whole, it is up to you to decide what your horse wears at a show, there are one or two restrictions on the type of equipment that can be used in competitions. They mostly apply to very severe gadgets which no decent rider would use anyway, but if you are planning to compete at affiliated shows it is advisable to check the rules beforehand. For instance, hackamores and other bitless bridles are permitted under British Show Jumping Association rules for horses but *not* for ponies.

NOSEBANDS

You may find, especially as your horse gets fitter, that you need a stronger noseband than a simple cavesson to help to give you more control by exerting pressure on the horse's nose, and also to prevent him from resisting by opening his mouth or crossing his jaw.

There are several options. Many people resort to the drop noseband but on some horses this is quite difficult to fit correctly and can interfere with the horse's breathing because it rests too close to the nostrils. A better alternative is the Grakle, first designed for a Grand National winner of that name. This has two straps which cross in the middle over the horse's nose. One fastens above the bit, the other below it.

A standing martingale should never be attached to a Grakle, so if you use this type of martingale you will need a flash noseband instead, which is basically a cavesson noseband with two crossing straps attached to the centre. These straps fasten below the bit in the same way as the lower halves of a Grakle.

MARTINGALES

A **running martingale** is a useful piece of equipment for the show jumper. It consists of a broad strap with a loop through which the girth passes. This strap is fitted between the horse's forelegs, passes through a neck strap and then divides in two. At the end of these thinner straps are rings through which the reins pass.

This martingale helps to prevent the horse from raising his head so high that you lose control. Correctly fitted, it does not come into action while the horse is carry-ing his head in the normal position. However, if he puts his head up in the air, the martingale exerts pressure on the reins and therefore on the bit. The martingale should not be fitted so tightly that it pulls down on the reins when the horse is carrying his head correctly.

As a safety precaution, you should always fit 'stops' on your reins if you use a running martingale. A rein stop is a small piece of leather or rubber with a slot in the middle through which the rein is passed. The stop is pushed down the rein and positioned between the bit and the martingale ring.

Grakle noseband.

Incorrectly fitted running martingale: the martingale should not come into action on the reins when the horse's head is in the correct position.

Standing martingale and flash noseband.

Boots

It is very easy for a horse to strike into himself with one of his own feet when he is jumping, so he should always be fitted with protective boots.

Overreach boots

Always use overreach boots to protect the horse's front feet. They guard against the heels of the forefeet being injured by the toes of the hind feet. Such injuries (overreaches) are most likely to occur when jumping on heavy (muddy) ground when the horse sometimes literally becomes stuck in the mud and is unable to get his forefeet out of the way of his hind feet as

quickly as usual. Choose overreach boots that fasten with a strap. Those that have to be pulled over the horse's hoof can be difficult to get on and off.

Tendon boots

Protect the forelegs with tendon boots. These give support to the tendons as well as protecting the back of the forelegs from blows from the hind feet.

Brushing boots

Use brushing boots on the hind legs if your horse tends to brush (knock his fetlock joints against each other).

Stops prevent the rings from becoming caught on some protruding part of the bridle, such as the buckles of the reins, or even on a horse's tooth.

The **standing martingale**, a single strap attached to the girth at one end and the cavesson noseband at the other and kept in place by a neckstrap, is also designed to stop the horse putting his head too high in the air. It can be useful on a horse with very bad head carriage but it is best avoided if possible because it can prevent the horse from stretching out his head and neck when jumping. In fact, under international jumping rules the standing martingale is not permitted.

STUDS

Studs are some of the most vital pieces of show jumping equipment.

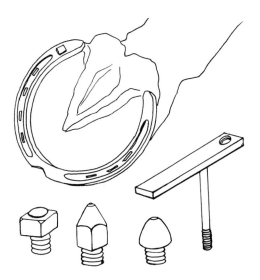

Studs come in different shapes for different types of ground conditions. The stud holes are kept clean with a stud tap (right).

They are screwed into holes, specially provided for this purpose by the farrier, in the horse's shoes. They help to prevent the horse from slipping when he is jumping. Having his feet slide from under him as he takes off at a fence is a frightening experience for a horse and may not only cause injury but also put him off jumping. Studs are particularly important when you are jumping out of doors where ground conditions vary so much.

Pointed studs give the best grip on dry, hard ground. The squarer the stud, the better the grip it will give when conditions are wet. Take a set of different studs with you to every show so that you will be prepared for a change in weather conditions. Of course you should also always use them when schooling at home.

Always remove the studs after jumping and protect the holes in the shoes by plugging them with oiled cotton wool when you are not using studs. Check the holes regularly, clean them out carefully and replug them. If you damage the screw thread, you won't be able to fit the studs again.

There are two views about how many studs to use. Many people fit just one on the outside of each shoe. Others believe that this can cause the horse's hoof to bear down unevenly on the ground, putting strain on the foot and leg, so they put a stud on both sides of each shoe.

Both methods seem to work equally well. The danger of using studs on the inside edge of the shoe is that the horse could injure himself by knocking, say, the inside of his near foreleg with the inside stud of his off fore. As with so many things concerned with horses, it is a matter of personal choice.

PRACTICE FENCES

You will need a selection of poles, stands and 'fillers' to practise over at home. Half a dozen poles will get you started, although you will need more when you come to build a succession of fences.

Ready-made poles come in assorted sizes and colours, or you can make your own from suitable timber. They should be at least 10 cm (4 in) in diameter and at least 3–3.6 m (10–12 ft) long – wide fences are easier to jump than narrow ones because they look much more inviting to a horse. If you make your own poles, be sure to take off any rough edges to prevent injury. Paint the poles in bright colours to resemble those you see at shows.

To support the poles, purpose-built wing stands are best because they are usually very solid-looking and stable. They are fitted with safe, easily adjustable metal or plastic cups on which the poles rest. If you cannot afford to buy stands, it is possible to construct them at home by copying professionally made ones. You can also buy specially designed synthetic blocks, which stack on each other, or even use oil drums so long as they are strong and free from rust.

Practice jumps should look as much like the real thing as possible and they must be *safe*. Never build fences with flimsy bits of old wood or rusty metal. They can break easily and cause injury and, anyway, horses never respect such obstacles and soon start jumping carelessly. Show jumps should look solid even though they are built to knock down easily.

Fillers – materials such as brush fences, little walls, wooden panels or planks – are important, too. They are used to make fences look more solid to the horse and they have the added benefit of making a course look attractive and varied to spectators.

If your horse has been taught to jump but has not done a great deal of competing, he might be taken by surprise by a new, unusual-looking fence at a show and stop for a closer look. This is why it is important to school over as many different obstacles as possible.

Fillers are not difficult to construct at home but, again, they must be absolutely safe. Barrels or drums painted in bright colours and laid end to end make a cheap type of filler, as do straw bales. In the interests of safety, always use a wedge or a peg in the ground to prevent barrels from rolling out of place and, if you use straw bales, make sure that they are tightly

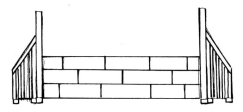

A wall with wings is a good, solid-looking obstacle.

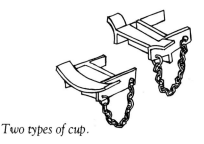

Two types of cup.

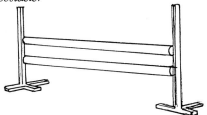

This simple vertical would be more inviting to the horse if it had a groundline.

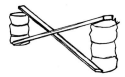

Avoid rusty oil drums and flimsy pieces of wood.

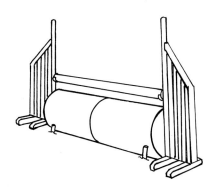

Rails over oil drums make a useful practice fence. The pegs prevent the drums from rolling.

packed so that there is no chance of the horse catching his foot in the baler twine if he makes a mistake.

A plank of wood, painted with different coloured patterns and placed under the top pole or poles of a fence, will also help to accustom a horse to unusual-looking fences.

TRAINING AREA

Choose a flat, well-drained area of ground, free from stones or other obstructions, for jumping training purposes. Avoid jumping when the ground is rock hard or very muddy. The less strain put on your horse's legs and feet at home, the longer he will go on competing.

In wet weather, move your jumps about regularly from one part of the field to another, to avoid cutting up the ground too much. Remember that it takes time for grassland to recover.

Clothes for the Rider

A hat with a chin harness and riding boots with smooth soles and a small heel are the two most important items of clothing for the rider.

A skull cap manufactured to British Standard 4472 (the type of headgear worn by jockeys) gives the best protection in the event of a fall. *Always wear your hat when practising at home.*

If you ride in jodhpurs or trousers at home (rather than breeches with long boots), wear jodhpur boots with them. They are better than shoes because they give protection to the ankles. Never ride in trainers, Wellington boots or other footwear with a ridged sole or no heel.

Riding boots are specially designed to prevent your foot becoming trapped by slipping through the stirrup iron or otherwise getting caught up in it in the event of a fall. Getting 'hung up' by one leg is every rider's nightmare – if the horse were to gallop off you would be dragged along with your head on the ground and probably under his back legs. *Never be tempted to ride in unsafe shoes.*

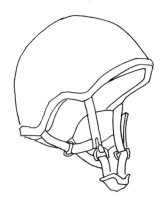
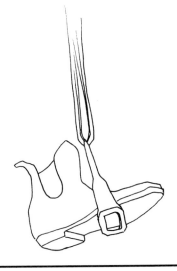

Two essential items of equipment for the rider: a skull cap fitted with a chin harness and riding boots with a heel.

Competition Dress

At shows it is a courtesy to the organizers and spectators to be as well turned out as possible. Always wear a neat shirt with a tie or stock, a well-fitting jacket that doesn't restrict your movement when you are jumping, breeches and boots, or jodhpurs and jodhpur boots.

If you jump at BSJA shows, your dress must conform to the requirements laid out in their rule book, which include wearing a white shirt (with a white tie or stock) if you wear a black or blue coat rather than a tweed one. Junior BSJA members who are also in the Pony Club may wear a Pony Club tie whatever the colour of their coat. Women may wear high-collared, white show jumping shirts without a tie or stock.

The BSJA strongly recommends that riders wear a BS4472 jockey skull cap, although they also permit a traditional riding cap provided it is made to standard BS6473. If you wear a skull cap, you should fit a plain dark-coloured silk (with a peak) over it when competing. All hats must be fitted with a retaining harness secured to the shell at more than two points and the harness must be correctly adjusted and fastened when you are mounted, whether you are in the arena, the practice area or the collecting ring.

Breeches and jodhpurs should be fawn, pale yellow or white.

You may need gloves if it is very cold or wet. Cotton, string and nylon are all suitable but leather becomes slippery in the wet.

CHAPTER 3

PRELIMINARY WORK ON THE FLAT

For many people, jumping is the most exciting part of riding. Whether you compete at international level or in your local riding club shows, there is the same sense of exhilaration and achievement to be derived from completing a stylish clear round over a course of fences.

Most riders find learning to jump rather difficult. The beginner tends to be thrown off balance by the thrust of power from the horse's hindquarters as he takes off, and finds it difficult, if not impossible, to regain that balance until the horse has landed again. It is because sitting on a horse over a fence gives such a different sensation to other forms of riding that it is so important to take things step by step: to practise over poles on the ground and then progress to very small obstacles before attempting anything too ambitious.

Trying to jump too much too soon will result, at best, in your losing confidence and, at worst, in the horse receiving painful jabs in the mouth as you try to keep your balance by hanging on to the reins.

Remember that riding with good style actually makes the horse's job easier.

ARE YOU READY TO JUMP?

You should not attempt to jump until you have developed a secure seat on a horse, totally independent of the reins, at all the different paces on the flat and have learned how to use the various aids – hands, legs, seat and so on – to control the horse.

You must be able to stay in balance with your horse, sitting up straight and relaxed with your head high. Your legs should be supple, not tense, and the lower part of your leg should lie naturally against the horse's side just behind the girth. You should not feel it necessary to grip tightly with your legs the entire time but should be at ease in the saddle whatever you ask your horse to do.

WHY DRESSAGE?

Many riders, who like the thought of going to shows to compete in jumping classes, are inclined to think of dressage as boring and, in the case of the show jumper, unnecessary. However, the truth is that you cannot expect to succeed in this sport if you neglect your horse's training on the flat.

Once a horse has learnt to jump correctly, he is unlikely to forget how. It is interesting to note that many famous international riders say they give their top horses very little schooling over fences between shows: just a few warm-up jumps before a competition is all that most of them require. It is not endless jumping practice but regular schooling on the flat that keeps them fit, supple and in the right outline to perform well in the ring.

It is, after all, the approach (in other words how he moves on the flat) that determines how well the horse will actually jump when he gets to the fence.

To jump successfully the horse needs to approach his fences calmly but in a good rhythm and with plenty of impulsion – that is, he must be going forward from the rider's leg, to a controlling hand, with his hind legs well under him. This 'compression' of power between the rider's leg and hand

The correct seat at the halt for work on the flat.

(rather like a tightly coiled spring) makes the horse's action more elevated and his whole outline shorter, giving him maximum spring when he reaches the take-off point at a fence.

Basic dressage develops the horse's balance, rhythm and impulsion and teaches him straightness, the correct bend on a circle and how to lengthen and shorten his stride on request – all essential skills for the show jumper.

WORK ON TURNS AND CIRCLES

During the course of a show jumping competition, you will be required to change direction several times. In a jump-off against the clock, the ability, or otherwise, to turn quickly can mean the difference between winning and losing. It is therefore essential that your horse can bend equally well to left or right and that you know how to ride him round a turn without having him fall out of balance or lose his impulsion.

Like human beings, horses tend to be born 'one-sided'. In the case of humans, this is manifested mainly in right- or left-handedness. With horses it appears as stiffness on one side of the body. Working your horse on circles and elements of circles will enable you to supple him up on his stiff side by building up the muscles until they are as well developed as those on his good side. Eventually, he should bend equally well on either rein.

Having achieved this suppleness, you can only maintain it by continuing to work him through the same school exercises described here throughout his career, otherwise he will tend to become one-sided again. Think of suppling exercises as the equivalent of the limbering-up work that all human athletes, gymnasts and dancers have to do every day if they are to stay fit.

Start by practising **turns** (at a good active rising trot) in the corners of your schooling area. If the horse is stiff on one side, work on his *supple* side first and only ask him to bend on his stiff side when he is well warmed up. Trying to force him into a position he is not physically able to achieve is not the answer.

As you approach a corner, put your weight a little more on your inside seat bone. Keep your shoulders parallel to the horse's shoulders – don't allow your outside shoulder to swing back and don't lean inwards. Your inside leg should be against the girth and your outside leg a little behind the girth to prevent the horse from swinging his quarters out to the side.

Give and take slightly with the inside rein (a dead pull on this rein will simply cause the horse's neck muscles to stiffen). The action of the outside rein is very important too. Although your hand must move forward to allow the horse's neck to bend to the inside, it must, at the same time, maintain a steady contact with the horse's mouth, otherwise he will probably bend just his neck and not his body.

The pony correctly bent on a turn in the corner of the school.

An incorrect turn: the pony's head is turned away from the direction of travel and the rider's inside hip has 'collapsed'.

Make sure that the horse does not slacken his pace but keeps moving forward actively. When you ride this movement correctly, the horse will bend his whole body as he negotiates the corner.

A horse does not have a great deal of lateral (sideways) flexion in his body but good training enables him to develop what he does have until he can travel on a **circle** with his hind legs following in the track of his forelegs. To do this, he has to bend his inside hind leg more than

when working on a straight line. It will, of course, take longer to achieve the correct bend on the horse's stiff side than on his more supple side.

When you work on circles, keep them large to begin with, not less than 20 m in diameter (the smaller the circle the more difficult it is for the horse to achieve the correct degree of bend). Once you can execute turns and large circles correctly at a good rhythmic trot, repeat the same exercises at canter,

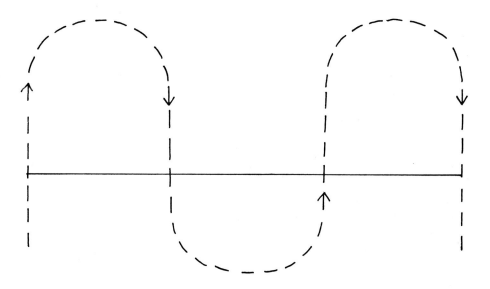

A three-loop serpentine helps to make the horse bend to both sides.

again taking great care to keep the horse balanced and going forward but with a nice bouncy, rhythmic stride and well under control.

As you become more proficient, you can gradually decrease the size of your circles. Small circles, down to a diameter of 10 m, should be ridden at sitting trot and you should use your seat to send the horse forward into a light, resisting hand. The horse's pace should be slower and rather more collected than when working on large circles, but his action should still be rhythmic and full of impulsion.

SERPENTINES

One of the best exercises you can practise, first at walk and then at rising trot, is the serpentine. This consists of riding three equal-sized loops, starting at one end of your schooling area and finishing at the other. It is an excellent means of making the horse bend to both sides alternately. When you want to change the direction of the bend, make sure that the horse goes straight for a couple of strides before giving him the aids to turn in the new direction.

When your horse is really supple, you can ask him to do more than three loops – the more you do the tighter the turns will be – and you can sit to the trot. Remember that it is best not to do sitting trot at the beginning of a schooling session but to wait until the horse's back muscles have had time to loosen up.

STRAIGHTNESS

A horse that can move in a straight line, with his hind feet following exactly in the tracks of his forefeet, is going to be a better athlete than one that goes crooked, with his hindquarters swinging out to one side or his head at an angle.

Because horses tend to be naturally one-sided, they have to be *taught* straightness and it is easier for them to move straight if they have first been made equally supple on both sides – hence the importance of work on circles and serpentines.

If you don't know whether your horse is straight, try riding him (on a straight line and on a circle) on a freshly raked surface in a school, then go and examine the hoof marks.

It is easier to achieve straightness with a horse that is moving strongly forward with impulsion. You will therefore find it easier to keep him straight at a good swinging trot than at a walk. It's the same principle as trying to ride a bicycle in a straight line: the slower you go the harder it becomes.

Remember, too, that one-sided riding can encourage a horse to be one-sided. If you have a continuing problem with your horse being crooked, it might be your fault, not his. Ask a good instructor to check that you are sitting straight, giving the aids to the horse correctly and not using one hand or leg more strongly than the other.

LENGTHENING AND SHORTENING THE STRIDE

When you ride over closely grouped fences, such as in a double or treble combination, there will be times when you need to lengthen or shorten your horse's stride to enable him to arrive at the right take-off point. The horse's ability to lengthen or shorten depends on longitudinal (lengthways) suppleness, as opposed to the lateral (sideways) suppleness he needs to negotiate turns.

Longitudinal suppleness is developed by practising transitions. A transition is a change of pace (for instance from walk to trot, or from trot to canter) or a change from one length of stride to another length of stride at the same pace (for instance from collected trot to extended trot).

Start by practising the transition from walk to trot. On a well-schooled horse, a squeeze from your legs should be sufficient to send him forward into trot. If it does not, carry a schooling whip and use this to tap the horse's side just behind your lower leg. If you use a proper schooling whip (about 90 cm or 3 ft long), you can do this without taking your hand off the rein. A tap with the whip is far better than endless thumping with your heels, which will eventually deaden the horse's sides to the aids. The horse will soon realize what is wanted and then you can dispense with the whip.

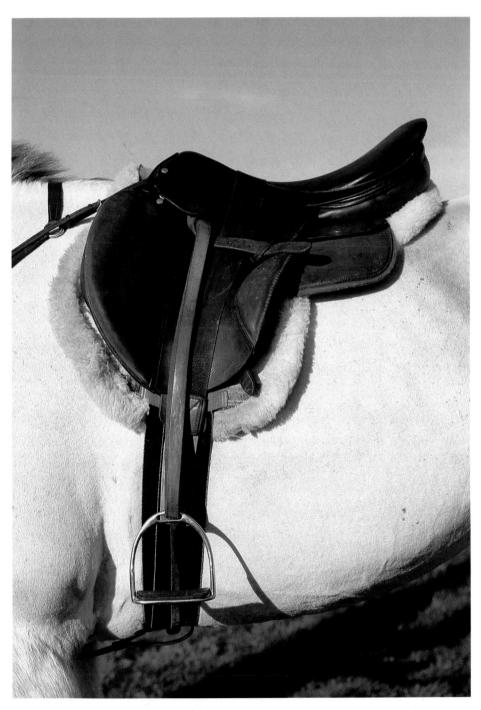

A forward-cut jumping saddle fitted with surcingle and numnah. It is easier to adopt a good position over a fence on this type of saddle, though many people learn to jump on a general purpose saddle.

Above: A young rider and pony neatly turned out for a competition.

Below: Work on a circle, an essential suppling exercise for the show jumper.

A good square halt.

Riding down a grid of poles on the ground at a good active trot.

Riding over raised trotting poles is an excellent exercise for improving your balance.

The first jump over a small cross-pole fence. Note the neck strap, a safety precaution in case the rider is 'left behind'.

The rider is showing a good leg position for take-off, although her hands should be maintaining contact with the pony's mouth.

Above: A correctly positioned grid and cross-pole fence enable horse and rider to tackle a second jump in good balance.

Below: Riding without stirrups is a good test of an independent seat!

Above: Jumping a single fence, the first step towards tackling a small course.

Below: The horse should be accustomed to jumping brightly coloured fences before you start competing.

Leaning to one side and looking down are faults which unbalance the horse.

Another common fault: the lower leg has swung back, making the rider insecure in the saddle.

Above: A poor jumping position. The rider has been seriously left behind, although she has managed to avoid jabbing the pony in the mouth.

Below: Most refusals are the result of rider error.

This horse has anticipated the next fence and is rushing towards it with his head up, which will put him out of balance at take-off.

V-shaped guide rails help keep the pony straight. Great care must be taken that they do not jam the pole into the cups. Ideally the horizontal pole should be resting on the *edge* of the cup so that if the pony hits it, it will easily fall.

Napping. Some horses start to nap because they dislike leaving their companions in the collecting ring. Patient re-schooling is essential.

Walking the course is a crucial part of show jumping. Walk each fence in the correct order and plan how you will approach them and where you will make your turns.

Reward your horse or pony after he has jumped his round and allow him to relax on a long rein.

On a cold day cover your pony with a rug and walk him about to keep him supple while waiting for a jump-off.

There are many ringside distractions at shows. Remember to give your horse plenty of time to look around and get used to them before taking him into the arena.

**The rider has prepared the horse to turn in the air over the fence
to save time.**

Above: The ability to make a tight turn to a fence can mean the difference between success and failure in a jump-off.

Below: Jumping at an angle is another good way to save valuable seconds in a jump-off.

Turning the competition horse out in his paddock on a regular basis helps him relax, but always fit boots or bandages to guard against injury.

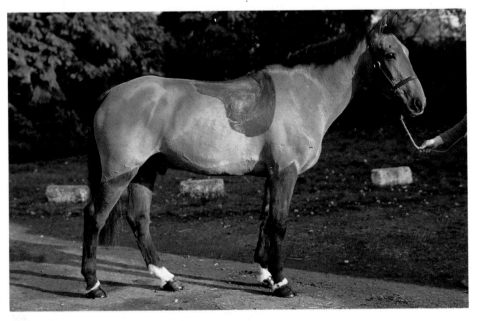

If he is to go indoor jumping in the winter, the horse will need a hunter clip. Always leave a saddle patch to protect his back.

Left: When doing roadwork always keep your horse going forward and straight. Protective boots, especially kneeboots, are a sensible precaution.

Below: Setting off up a stiffish hill at a brisk trot. Hillwork is one of the best ways of getting a horse fit. Note the protective boots on the horse's forelegs.

A downward transition is more difficult to do well than an upward one because it is easier for the horse to fall out of balance and to lose impulsion. Sit deep in the saddle, with your body upright. Don't think of the transition merely as a pull on the reins. Keep your legs firmly on the horse's sides to ensure that his hind legs remain well under him. Think of it as riding him forward into a lightly resisting hand; that is, one that ceases momentarily to follow the movement of his head and neck. When you get it right the transition will be smooth, not jerky, and the horse will not lose his balance but will change pace without showing any signs of resistance. When you can make smooth transitions from walk to trot and back down again, start practising walk to trot to canter to trot to walk.

Having learned to do smooth transitions from one pace to another, try asking the horse to change the length of his stride within the same pace. Remember that going faster is not the same thing as lengthening the stride. It won't, for instance, help you to reach the right take-off point at the second part of a double if the distance between the two fences is a bit too long for your horse.

Start by riding at a good 'working' trot. This pace will be like your horse's natural trot, although your regular schooling sessions should have made it rather more active. Riding in rising trot, use soft pressure from your legs as your seat is in the saddle and, at the same time, give the horse a fraction more rein so that he can extend his head and neck. He should start to take longer strides, although his speed will increase only marginally. If he simply goes faster, start again. Depending on your horse's level of training, it may take a little time before your get extension, not speed. Be patient, keep repeating the exercise until you get it right.

When the horse achieves extension, keep it going for a few strides, then go back to working trot by stopping your leg aid and closing your fingers on the reins. You will find it easier in sitting trot, because you can use your seat to push the horse forward, but don't do a lot of work at sitting trot until your horse's back is well muscled up.

Finally, practise lengthening and shortening the stride at canter, the pace that you will use when actually show jumping. As always, the golden rule is that the horse must first have his hindquarters engaged; that is, his hocks must be well underneath him to enable him either to propel himself forwards or to shift more weight on to his hind legs allowing him to shorten his stride. If they aren't, he will merely start 'running', with his weight on his forehand and his strides simply becoming faster rather than longer.

The best way to ensure that the horse's quarters are engaged is to make use of the half-halt.

Going from trot to canter. Smooth transitions from one pace to another develop longitudinal suppleness.

PRACTICAL SHOWJUMPING

The Half-halt

The half-halt is a momentary check used by the rider to adjust the horse's balance and to encourage him to put more of his weight on his hindquarters. It also prepares him mentally for a new set of aids, for instance when the rider wants to change pace or direction. Repeated half-halts are a good way of calming an excitable horse.

As with jumping, it is difficult, if not impossible, for the novice rider to learn how to ask for a half-halt on an unschooled horse, so make sure your horse has been taught it before your start practising, otherwise you will both become confused.

If you have never tried a half-halt before, start at walk. The aids are the same as those for halt, but the strength with which you apply them will vary depending on how much you want the horse to react, how sensitive he is and how quickly he responds.

To ask for a half-halt, close your legs against the horse's sides to send him forward, and sit deeply in the saddle. As you do this, you should feel the horse going forward more strongly into the reins. Immediately this happens, give a momentary squeeze on the reins instead of following the horse's forward movement with your hands. The important

point is that the whole thing should be *momentary*. When it is well performed, the half-halt is barely noticeable to the spectator. If the horse stops with a jolt, your aids have been too strong; he has misunderstood and thinks you wanted him to halt. If he starts to pull and lean on the bit, your leg aids have been too strong. All he should do is bend his hind legs more, lower his quarters and shift his weight further back, while still continuing to move rhythmically forward.

To understand what you are asking the horse to do, try watching steeplechasing on television. Look out for a riderless horse who continues to gallop and jump with his rivals. As he approaches a fence he will shift his weight back onto his hindquarters in the stride before he takes off. You can see this most clearly in slow motion. The horse knows instinctively that what the rider calls a half-halt is the best way of preparing himself to jump a big obstacle. All the rider has to do is to train the horse to perform a half-halt on request.

Once you get the feel of the half-halt at walk, practise it at the faster gaits. When you come to compete over show jumps, you will find it a most useful means of balancing a horse during the approach to a fence.

POINTS TO REMEMBER

U The better your horse is schooled on the flat, the better he will become at show jumping.

U Don't neglect your schooling: even if you are just out hacking you can practise the half-halt, transitions, lengthening and shortening the stride and correct turns.

U Don't ask the horse to perform difficult movements, and don't ride in sitting trot, until he is well warmed up.

U Work the horse first on his more supple side, then on his stiffer side, never the other way round.

U Always finish your schooling session on a good note, with a movement that has been performed well. Let your horse know that you are pleased with him by giving him a pat and a word of praise and let him relax by walking on a long rein.

U Never start jumping until you have done some flatwork to supple up your horse's muscles, to get him balanced and full of impulsion.

U If you can't seem to get a particular movement right, however much you practise, ask for expert help. It's surprising how quickly a good instructor can solve a seemingly insuperable problem.

CHAPTER 4

THE FORWARD SEAT

Once you have developed a balanced seat on the flat, totally independent of the reins, you can confidently begin to think about your first jumping lessons.

The best way to start is on a calm, experienced horse under the eye of a good instructor. That way, the rider has the best chance of learning how to sit correctly and avoid developing bad habits. Beginners should not be tempted to go out into a field on their own, aim the horse at a fence and hope for the best. You might not fall off but the chances are that you won't ride very well either! Some riders never learn to jump in good style – usually because they have hurried their basic training.

Take things one step at a time. Start by studying the differences between the basic position you have been taught on the flat and the position you need to adopt when jumping . Then practise riding in the jumping or forward seat on the flat.

Next, try working over poles on the ground. Only when you can do that in good balance and without having to use the reins as a lifeline, should you progress to your first little jumps.

THE JUMPING SEAT

The first step is to understand the importance of the rider's basic position when jumping and how it differs from that used on the flat.

The jumping or forward seat is designed to enable you to 'go with' the horse during all the various

Practising the forward-inclined jumping seat at halt. The rider should not allow the lower leg to swing back.

phases of the jump – the approach, the take-off, the actual flight through the air, the landing and the get-away.

It involves shortening your stirrups by two or three holes, which enables you to ride with your weight further forward than on the flat. This weight adjustment is necessary because the horse's centre of balance shifts further forward when he travels at fast paces and when he jumps. If the rider gets behind the movement, it will affect the horse's balance and make his job of jumping fences much more difficult.

To stay in balance with a horse when jumping, you must incline the upper half of your body forwards. When riding on the flat your shoulders should be in line with your hips but when jumping they should be in advance of your hips. Shortening your stirrups has the effect of closing the angle between your body and thigh, making it easier for you to achieve this forward position.

Instead of your weight being directly on your seatbones, it will now be transferred, through your thighs and knees, more onto the balls of your feet in the stirrup irons. This removal of weight from the horse's back makes the task of clearing a fence far simpler for him than if you were to remain sitting upright in the saddle.

When jumping, your security in the saddle depends on balance and a good leg position. In the forward seat, your lower leg should be close to the horse's side, directly underneath you, with your ankle flexed

and your toe up. You should feel your weight going down into your heel.

The best way to practise the jumping seat is at trot and canter on the flat. Until you can stay in balance in the forward position at both paces, you are not ready for jumping.

POLES ON THE GROUND

Riding over poles on the ground is an excellent way of developing balance in the forward seat. Start by placing individual poles around your schooling area. To begin with, walk the horse over them, making sure that your hands follow the movement of his head and neck as he stretches forward. Remember that your body should be inclined slightly forward so that your shoulders are in advance of your hips. Then try going over the poles at rising trot.

The next step is to make a little grid of three poles, about 1.4 m (4 ft 6 in) apart. The distance must be adjusted to suit your particular horse's stride and this is where an assistant comes in useful. It is foolish to begin jumping practice without someone nearby to help in the event of an accident and, far from standing on the sidelines, this helper can prove indispensable in moving poles about, adjusting the size of fences and so on.

Walk back and forth over this grid until you can maintain your forward position without difficulty, then ride over it at rising trot.

Maintaining the jumping seat at trot with the weight well down in the heel.

The jumping seat at canter.

Concentrate on keeping the upper part of your body inclined forward, your lower leg in the correct position and a straight line from your elbow, via your hand, to the horse's mouth. Again, remember that you must follow the horse's head and neck movements with your hands. Gradually add more poles to the grid until you are going confidently down a line of six poles.

When you feel comfortable doing this exercise at rising trot, try it at sitting trot. To do this well requires increased suppleness as well as good balance.

Now raise the poles a little off the ground – 15–23 cm (6–9 in) is sufficient. This can be done by putting blocks or bricks under the ends. Or, if you have them, you can use cavalletti, set at their lowest height. As he trots over the raised poles, the horse will bend his knees and hocks more and, again, this is an excellent exercise for improving your balance.

Trotting over poles without stirrups also greatly improves the rider's balance and strengthens the seat.

THE FIRST JUMP

The easiest way to become accustomed to the sensation of actually jumping is to use a small cross-pole fence, about 38 cm (15 in) high, at the end of a line of trotting poles or low cavalletti. Depending on the horse's stride, the fence should be placed about 2.7–3 m (9–10 ft) from the final pole. The poles

---

Ten Common Rider Faults

All of the following commonly seen faults of style make it more difficult for the horse to stay in balance and jump well:

U Dropping the reins (losing contact) during the last few strides.

U Leaning too far forward during the approach.

U Taking off before the horse.

U Getting left behind at take-off.

U Leaning to one side over the jump.

U Looking down instead of ahead.

U Raising the heel above the level of the toe.

U Swinging the lower leg back.

U Using the horse's neck for support.

U Sitting back in the saddle with a bump on landing.

---

should be ridden as usual in trot.

The trotting poles ensure that the horse approaches the little fence in a controlled manner, and the use of a cross-pole fence helps to keep him straight. This leaves you free to concentrate on your position. It is all too easy at this stage to develop faults in your style, which is why it is so important to carry out this early practice with a good instructor on hand to point out where you are going wrong.

Stages of Jumping

The rider's chief aim when jumping is to give the horse the best chance of clearing the fence. This means bringing the horse in straight to the obstacle with rhythm, balance and impulsion and then interfering with him as little as possible by sitting still in the saddle and going with the movement. The various stages of the jump require different skills on the rider's part.

The Approach

During the approach to a fence, your weight should be channelled through your hips and knees onto the balls of your feet. Your lower legs should be directly under you and close against the horse's sides. Although your seatbones will be raised slightly out of the saddle, you should not lean forward in an exaggerated way, otherwise you will make it difficult for the horse to raise his shoulders when he takes off.

A good approach is the key to a good jump. Although the rider uses the forward seat, he or she must be ready to sit

deeper and more upright in the saddle when it is required during those last few strides. For instance, the horse might need to be checked with a half-halt or driven on with stronger seat and leg aids. The rider must learn to make these adjustments to his or her own position quickly and without unbalancing the horse.

The approach to a fence should always be *straight* and controlled. Keep the horse balanced and in a good rhythm by riding him forward from your legs and maintaining a steady contact with the reins. As he nears the fence, the horse will stretch out his neck and lower his head a little as he sizes up the obstacle and prepares for take-off. Your hands must follow this movement without dropping the contact.

The Take-off

As he gets ready to take off, the horse raises his head and neck and brings his hind legs well under him to push himself upwards. In order to give him full use of his back, you should take your weight out of the saddle at this moment.

One of the commonest faults is for the rider to take off before the horse; that is,

Approach   Take-off   Flight

The five stages of jumping, with the rider correctly positioned for each stage. Note the secure lower leg position and the straight line from the elbow.

to lean too far forward too soon. Coming forward before the horse gets his front legs off the ground does not help him, it merely puts extra weight on his forehand just as he is trying to get airborne.

Once his shoulders have come up, now is the time to lean further forward, bending from your hips. As always, you must follow the movement of his head with your hands.

Over the Fence

While the horse is airborne, you should sit still, with your seat just out of the saddle and your lower leg under you and close to the girth. If you allow your heels to come up or your whole lower leg to swing back, you will have a less secure seat. The chances are that you will pitch forward and end up using the horse's neck for support, which will interfere with his balance.

While in flight over the fence, you should sit straight, keep your head up and look forward. Leaning to one side, looking down or looking back all cause a shift of weight and, as a result, tend to unbalance the horse. Remember that your head is the heaviest part of your body, so riders, like other sportspeople, need to keep their heads as still as possible in order to avoid sudden shifts of balance.

The Landing

As the horse's forehand starts to descend in preparation for landing, gradually straighten your body but still keep your weight out of the saddle so that the horse has every opportunity to clear the fence with his hindquarters.

The impact of landing, which increases as the size of the fences increases, is absorbed through your hip, knee and ankle, which must all be supple.

The Getaway

Having touched down with his front feet, the horse brings his hind feet under him again and prepares to push himself forward into the first canter stride. At this point your upper body should have straightened and you should be back in the forward position adopted during the approach, ready to use your legs, and seat if necessary, to drive the horse forward to the next fence.

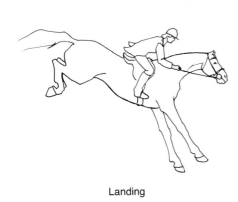

Landing

Getaway

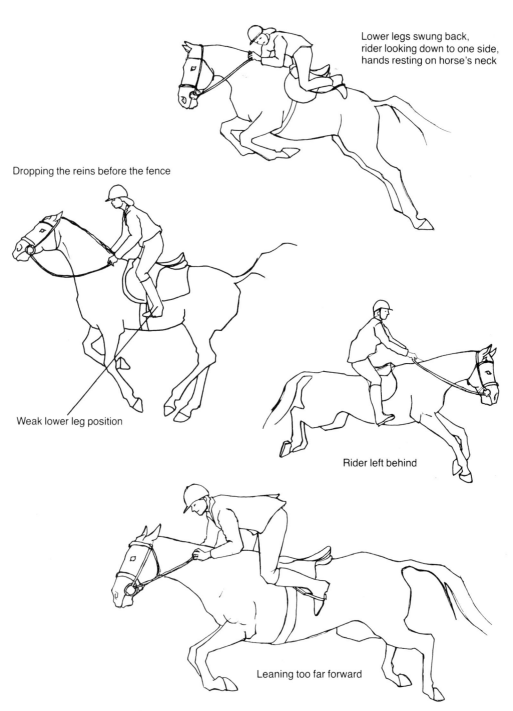

Lower legs swung back,
rider looking down to one side,
hands resting on horse's neck

Dropping the reins before the fence

Weak lower leg position

Rider left behind

Leaning too far forward

Some common faults.

The worst sin when learning to jump is to jab a horse in the mouth. To avoid this, many instructors take the precaution of fitting a neckstrap, which you can catch hold of in moments of emergency.

If you find no difficulty in coping with the little fence at the end of the trotting poles, try placing another one 5.5–6 m (18–21 ft) further on. This will allow the horse to take a canter stride between the two little jumps and will give you your first introduction to jumping from canter.

When the horse lands over these little fences, he will probably go on in canter. Let him take a few canter strides before asking him to come back to trot to do the exercise again. The getaway from a fence is important when you start competing and it is better to encourage the horse to get quickly into his stride after landing than to allow him to linger.

CHAPTER 5

GRIDS AND SIMPLE FENCES

Having mastered the basics of the forward seat over a line of poles followed by a small cross-pole fence or two, you should be ready to do more strenuous gymnastic jumping exercises to help to establish your position in the saddle.

Riding over grids of small fences is ideal for developing good balance and a secure seat. When built correctly, grids continue to make the horse's job simple, thus giving you every opportunity to concentrate on your style of riding. If you take the trouble to work on this aspect of jumping training in the early stages, you should graduate to tackling individual fences and, eventually, a small course, with no loss of confidence.

The golden rule is never to be in too much of a hurry: master one thing at a time.

GRIDWORK

Think of gridwork as an extension of the trotting-pole exercises. The chief difference is that the horse will now be coming up slightly further off the ground over the little jumps than he did over the poles or cavalletti, and he will be travelling

faster. In fact, jumping out of canter is more comfortable for the rider than jumping from trot, so there is no need to be alarmed by the prospect of jumping at a faster pace.

Begin by building three small fences (or you can use cavalletti set at their top height) after your trotting poles. If you use fences, make the first one a cross-pole and place it about 3 m (10 ft) from the last trotting pole. Put another little fence about 5.5–6.4 m (18–21 ft) beyond the cross-pole to allow the horse to take one canter stride between the two. A third fence placed 10–10.6 m (33–35 ft) after the second one will allow for two canter strides. By building this obstacle as a little spread fence, you can encourage the horse to make a slightly bigger effort and to round himself more. This will help to give you the feel of jumping bigger fences.

In time, one or two more little obstacles can be added to your grid. They may be placed at one or two canter strides from each other or you can vary things by introducing a 'bounce'. This is where the horse lands over one jump and takes off at the next without taking a stride. If a bounce is placed at the start of

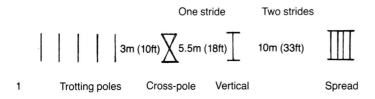

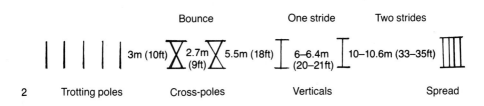

Grids suitable for novice horse and rider. The distances should be adjusted as necessary, depending on the horse.

the grid, which should still be approached in trot, the distance between the two bounce fences should be about 2.7 m (9 ft). In the middle of a grid, when the horse will be cantering, the distance for a bounce will need to be 3.6 m (12 ft).

If possible, introduce a small brush fence or a low wall into the line of fences, rather than using only poles. Varying the appearance of the fences will keep the horse alert and prevent boredom from setting in. However, always use fence material that knocks down easily. This is particularly important in grids, otherwise the horse

may frighten himself if he makes a mistake.

Regular practice over grids of this type, with the fences kept low, will soon give you the idea of what jumping is all about. As you become more confident, your instructor may well ask you to tackle such exercises without reins – a good test of whether or not you really have acquired a truly independent seat!

When you have, and can perform these exercises easily and without any suggestion of being 'left behind' or otherwise losing your balance, you will be ready to practise over single obstacles.

SINGLE FENCES

Jumping an individual fence is much more difficult than approaching an obstacle via a line of trotting poles. Trotting poles ensure that the horse cannot reach the fence anywhere but at the correct take-off point. Once they are removed, it is up to you to start planning the approach rather than concentrating solely on how you are sitting in the saddle.

To begin with, it is unlikely that you will always judge your approach correctly, so you may find your horse having to take off sooner than you expected or getting in closer than usual to the fence. This is when a secure seat is essential, so that you can 'go with' your horse even at slightly uncomfortable moments. Fences this small should prove no problem for the horse even if you do not give him a perfect approach but it would be very unfair of you to reward him by jabbing him in the mouth or having all your weight in the saddle at the wrong moment.

To help you progress from grids to single fences, it is a good idea to use placing poles. A placing pole is one that is positioned a little way in front of a fence to help the horse to arrive at the correct take-off point. Placing poles can be laid on the ground or raised slightly, or you can use cavalletti. To begin with, put the placing pole 2.7 m (9 ft) from the fence and approach at a good active trot, allowing the horse to go into canter on landing over the fence. Canter away from it.

Return to trot before attempting the exercise again. For a canter approach, put the placing pole 5.5 m (18 ft) from the fence to enable the horse to take one stride between the pole and fence. Vary things for your horse by setting up two or three jumps, each with a placing pole, in different parts of your schooling area.

Keep the fences small at this stage – 75–90 cm (2 ft 6 in–3 ft) is perfectly adequate. The object is to improve your riding, not to see how high your horse can jump. When you do feel that you are ready to tackle something larger, it is better to make the fences wider rather than higher. Spread fences encourage horses to jump in a good outline which, in turn, will improve your technique.

Remember to give the horse a groundline to help him judge his jump. A wall has its own groundline, while a rail 90 cm (3 ft) off the ground can be made much easier by placing a pole on the ground either immediately underneath it or slightly in front. Never give the horse a false groundline; that is, one that is further back than the top of the fence. It will confuse him and cause him to make mistakes.

When you are happy jumping these slightly larger single fences, try moving the placing poles further back so that they are about 13.7 m (45 ft) from the fences. Now your horse will be able to take three canter strides between the pole and the obstacle. This is the next step in accustoming you to

A placing pole on the ground makes this small spread fence an easy obstacle.

approaching fences at canter. Continue riding to each distance pole at trot so that there is no possibility of the horse rushing in an uncontrolled manner at the fences.

The final test is to try jumping little fences without the help of placing poles. To begin with, approach at trot – provided the fences are no more than 90 cm (3 ft) high, your horse should have no problem in clearing them. Then try approaching at a steady canter, remembering that it is a controlled, rhythmic pace that is required, not a flat-out gallop from halfway across the field.

FURTHER PRACTICE

There are many ways of improving your jumping skills before you attempt your first competition. Riding over grids made up entirely of bounces is an excellent suppling exercise for both rider and horse

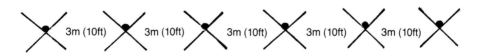

Riding down a bounce grid of cavalletti is an excellent suppling exercise.

Changes of Direction

If you start competing at all seriously, you will need to learn how to perform a flying change in order to cope with the various changes of direction called for in the average show jumping course without breaking your pace. This involves asking the horse to change his leading leg at canter.

To begin with, however, you can do things much more simply just by slowing down briefly from canter to trot and then setting off again on the new canter lead. A good way of practising this is to place four fences on a large figure of eight, with a placing pole 5.5 m (18 ft) in front of each fence.

Approach the first pole in trot, let the horse canter for a few strides after landing over the fence, then go back into trot before approaching the second fence. Repeat the process, making a wide turn (in trot) round to the third fence. Again, return to trot before riding to fence four. Having mastered this exercise, try moving some or all of the distance poles back to allow for three canter strides before the fences.

The next step is to remove the placing poles altogether from in front of fences two and four. These two fences should be positioned a measured number of horse strides (say seven or eight : one stride for a horse is 3.6 m or 12 ft; for a pony 2.7 m or 9 ft) after fences one and three. Trot to the distance pole in front of fence one, then canter on to fence two. Return to trot to negotiate the turn to fence three, trot to the placing pole then complete the exercise at canter.

Eventually, you can attempt all four fences at canter and without any placing poles. To change leg, come back to trot briefly after fence two and ask your horse to strike off on the other lead as you go into the turn. This is where schooling on the flat proves invaluable – a smooth downward transition to trot and another upward one back to canter, followed by a good turn, will ensure that the horse remains in balance and approaches the next fence still full of impulsion.

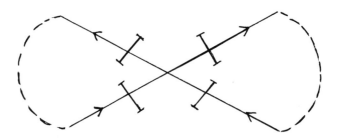

Jumping fences set on a figure of eight teaches both horse and rider how to cope with changes of direction.

and is something that can easily be practised at home. The grid can be made up of cavalletti set at their highest position or little fences no more than 46–60 cm (18–24 in) high. They should be set about 3 m (10 ft) apart so that there is no room for the horse to put in a stride. Start with a grid of three and build up gradually to six. The grid should be ridden at a steady canter.

The ultimate test is to ride the grid without reins or stirrups – although, for safety, this is best done in a confined area and under the supervision of an instructor.

Jumping on circles is another valuable exercise. It makes the horse supple and prepares both him and his rider for changes of direction.

Because it is more tiring than jumping on straight lines, it should be done for short periods only and the horse should always be worked on his more supple side first.

Put two or three poles in a fan shape on the ground on a 20 m circle. They should be about 1.2 m (4 ft) apart on the inside of the circle and 1.5–1.8 m (5–6 ft) apart on the outside, according to the horse's length of stride. Start by walking over the centre of the poles on either rein, then progress to a nice rhythmic trot. Gradually increase the number of poles to five or six.

In time, you can raise the poles off the ground a little or replace them with low cavalletti. When

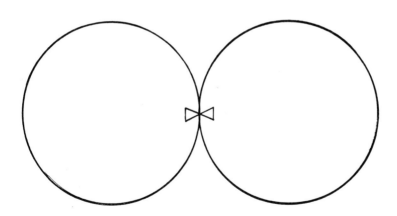

Jumping a cross-pole fence from circles encourages the horse to land on the correct canter lead.

you can perform this exercise in a good rhythm, let your horse come out of the grid at canter. If he is well balanced, he will almost certainly strike off on the correct leg; that is, the right leg if you are working on a circle to the right, and the left leg if you are circling to the left.

Next, place a small cross-pole fence in the centre of your school-ing area, parallel to the long sides. Practise riding circles of equal diameter, first to the left and then to the right, jumping the little fence where your two circles touch. Ride the first circle on the horse's more supple side in trot and, as he is going over the fence give the aids for canter. If you are circling to the right, use your right hand to turn

his head slightly inwards and your left leg behind the girth. As he lands and canters away, you should find that he is leading with his off fore.

Practise circles on both reins and then try a figure of eight. This involves riding on, say, a circle to the left and then, as the horse jumps the fence, applying the aids for the right canter lead. With practice, you should find that by indicating to the horse which direction you intend to go on land-ing, he will change leg in midair. Watch the professionals in action and you will see them get it right every time. The ability to have the horse land on the correct leading leg is a tremendous help when jumping a course.

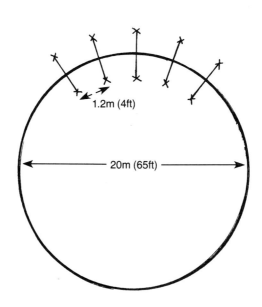

Jumps set out on a circle will help to make the horse supple.

TYPES OF FENCES

There are several different types of show jumping fence, each of which presents a particular problem for the horse and rider. Even in novice competitions the course builder will include a variety of different obstacles, so it is very important to practise over the various types at home so that you know how to ride them when you get to a show.

Upright fences

Upright fences are ones in which all the poles or planks are set in the same vertical plane, one immediately above the other. Walls and gates are also upright fences. Uprights are the most difficult for the horse to jump accurately. This

is because a horse judges his take-off point at a fence from the ground line (the base of the fence) and he is more likely to take off too close to an upright than to a sloping jump such as a triple bar.

To jump an upright successfully, the horse needs to reach the highest point of his leap exactly over the top of the obstacle. If he takes off too close, he is likely to hit the obstacle with his front legs. If he stands off too far, he will probably hit it with his back legs. When practising over uprights at home, you can make it easier for the horse by placing a pole on the ground slightly in advance of the fence.

Concentrate on making your approach as accurate as possible. The horse should come to the

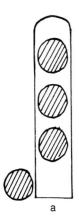 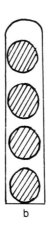 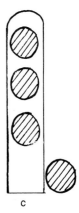

a   b   c

An upright fence of poles with three different groundlines: (a) easy; (b) less easy; (c) false.

fence absolutely straight and full of impulsion but not in a hurry. Keep the canter rhythmic and balanced and don't try to make last-minute adjustments which will merely unbalance the horse and, as likely as not, cause him to make a mistake.

Remember that when jumping an upright the horse's descent is steeper than when jumping a spread. This affects his getaway stride from the fence, making it rather short. When competing, you should take this into account when measuring distances between fences during the course walk.

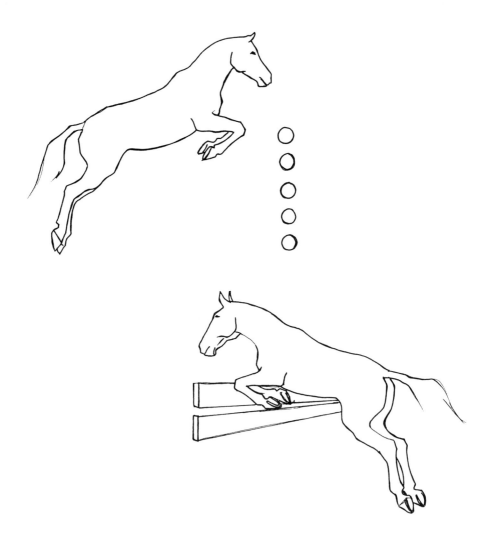

Top: *Horse standing off too far back: he is likely to hit the fence 'behind'*. Bottom: *Horse getting in too close: He will hit the fence 'in front'*.

Triple bar

A triple bar is known as a 'staircase fence' because of the way it is built, with the second and third rails progressively higher than the first. It is a much easier obstacle for a horse than an upright because it is the same shape as the arc that he makes as he jumps. He does not need to fold his front legs up quite as quickly as usual when he takes off, and he lands less steeply than over an upright, which enables him to take a longer getaway stride.

However, the horse does need plenty of impulsion to clear the width of the fence and he should be encouraged to take off quite close to the front rail. It helps if the rider focuses on the *middle* rail of a triple bar during the approach. That way

you are less likely to ask the horse to take off too soon.

Putting a filler, such as a hedge or wall, under the front rail makes the whole fence look more solid. This, in turn, will tend to make a horse back off more, so you need to ride at such a fence with extra impulsion to overcome any hesitation on the horse's part.

Ascending spread

An ascending spread fence has the front pole lower than the back pole and is an easier obstacle to jump than a true parallel. Horses need plenty of impulsion to clear all spread fences. However, although you need to drive the horse forward with your legs during the approach to such a jump, you must not let

The triple bar, also known as a 'staircase' fence.

An ascending spread is easier to jump than a true parallel.

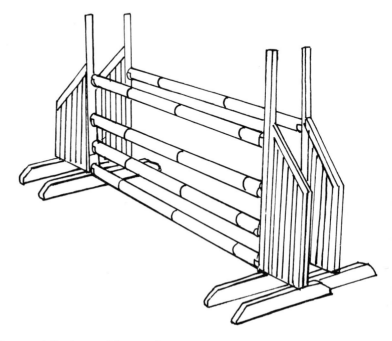

A true parallel is the most difficult spread fence to jump.

him increase his speed. If you do he will end up with too much weight on his forehand and will be unable to clear the fence. As with the triple bar, the horse must not take off too far away at a spread, otherwise he will not clear the back rail. On the other hand, he must not pick up so close that he knocks the front pole off with his knees or feet as he takes off.

When practising at home, build a variety of little spread fences to resemble those you may see at shows. If you have sufficient materials, use planks as well as poles for the front part, or a wall or brush fence with a rail over it. For safety, never use anything but a single pole for the back of any type of spread fence and never put a filler under it.

Parallel fences

Parallel or square fences have the back pole at the same height as the front one and are the most difficult of all spread fences as they test a horse's scope and jumping technique far more than ascending spreads. Even if he jumps a bit flat, a horse can often manage to clear an ascending spread, but at a parallel an accurate approach and good style in the air are vital.

You must make sure that the horse is well balanced, with his strides rhythmic and full of impulsion, as he approaches the obstacle. If he fails to fold his forelegs up quickly or dangles his back legs, he will hit the front pole. If he neglects to lift and stretch out his back legs during his flight over the fence, he will hit the back pole as he starts his descent.

Remember, when building parallel fences (and other spread fences), that there should never be a false groundline. For instance, a parallel consisting of rails in front, a back rail, and a brush fence in between as a filler (this fence is known as an oxer) is too difficult for a novice horse because he will use the base of the brush fence to judge his take-off and so get too close to the front of the fence.

If you want to construct a solid-looking jump of this kind, then put a filler under the front rail as well, to hide the base of any bushes used as a central filling.

Combination fences

Fences that are built so close together that there is room for only one or two strides between them are known as combinations. A double consists of two fences, a treble of three. In international-level show jumping, course builders may present extremely difficult problems just by the order in which they arrange the obstacles and the distances they put between them. For novices, however, the distances will be straightforward – provided the rider gets the approach to the first fence right!

Even at a very novice level you will find double combinations included in courses and it will not be long before you have to tackle simple trebles as well, so it makes sense to practise at home before you start competing.

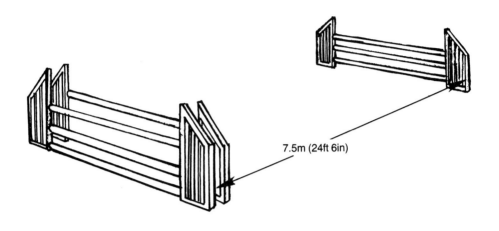

7.5m (24ft 6in)

A double comprising an ascending spread and an upright, set at the 'true' distance for one stride.

The most important factors are the types of fences used and the distances between them. It is essential that you learn how to measure out, using your own stride, combination distances in relation to your horse's stride. At novice level the course builder will use 'true' distances in combinations; that is, distances based on the average natural stride of a horse or pony. These are taken to be 3.6 m (12 ft) for a horse and 2.7 m (9 ft) for a pony.

In a double of two upright fences with one non-jumping stride between them, the 'true' distance for a horse is about 7.3 m (24 ft). This allows for the horse landing about 1.8 m (6 ft) beyond the first fence, putting in one normal canter stride and taking off about 1.8 m (6 ft) from the second fence. For two non-jumping strides, the distance will be about 10.5 m (34 ft 6 in).

Work out how long your own walking stride is – if you can, aim for 90 cm (3 ft) – and then practise 'walking' the distances between combination fences at home. Stand with your back against the landing side of the first fence and make sure you take even strides to the next one. You will find it easier to keep your strides the same

Learn to stride out distances in combinations at home in readiness for walking the course at shows.

length if you look at the ground, not at the next fence.

If your horse has a shorter than average stride, then you will know that in a 7.3 m (24 ft) double you will have to lengthen his stride in order to meet the second fence at the correct take-off point. If he has a longer than average stride, you will have to be careful not to allow him to jump in too far over the first fence and you must be prepared to ask him to shorten between the two obstacles.

Build simple double and treble combinations at home to practise over. Measure the distances carefully and only use uprights, ascending spreads and small parallels. Triple bars in combinations are too difficult for novice horses. If you build a spread fence followed by an upright, you must make the distance slightly longer (about 7.5 m or 24 ft 6 in) because the horse will land further out over the first fence than he would when jumping an upright. If you build an upright followed by a spread, or two spreads, reduce the distance slightly.

Remember that a number of things will affect the length of a horse's stride. If the ground is muddy, his stride may shorten by as much as 30 cm (1 ft). The same

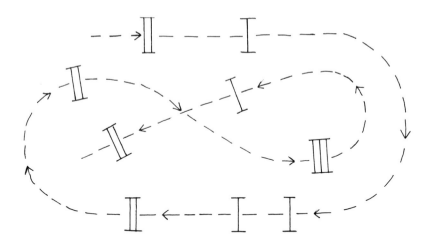

A simple course to practise over at home; remember to start with a small ascending spread and to include a simple double and changes of direction.

thing happens when jumping uphill or in a confined space such as an indoor arena.

A horse usually shortens his stride when going away from home, too – in the case of a competition this means away from the collecting ring. The reverse will happen; that is, his stride may lengthen by up to 30 cm (1 ft) on good ground, when going slightly downhill and when jumping in a large arena or in the direction of home.

Good course builders take account of these factors at shows and you should do the same when constructing practice fences at home.

BUILDING A COURSE

Before you compete at a show it is best to practise riding a small course a few times. If you have enough equipment available try to build about eight or ten fences, including at least one double. Start with an easy ascending spread to give the horse confidence and then vary the types of fences between uprights and spreads, including a triple bar. Make them as solid-looking as possible. Include changes of direction but avoid sharp, awkward turns. Try to make the whole course 'flowing' so that you can keep going in a good rhythm.

CHAPTER 6

COMMON PROBLEMS

A good rider on a well-trained horse should not encounter too many difficulties when jumping. However, as with all aspects of horsemanship, things may not always go exactly according to plan and you are bound to come up against the odd problem from time to time.

Most problems, such as refusals and run-outs, are caused by rider error. It may be that you are making a basic mistake in the signals you are giving to your horse, or are asking him to progress too quickly in his training. Perhaps you have simply inherited a problem caused by the horse's previous owner. Whatever the difficulty, you must work out what is causing it, taking advice from a more experienced person if necessary, and then set about curing it. This invariably means going back to basic training. Short cuts and gadgets rarely work.

RUSHING

Cause

Horses who speed up the moment they see a fence in front of them are often thought to be over eager and the novice rider's instinctive reaction is to try to achieve a more controlled approach by hauling on the reins. In fact, the problem of rushing is usually caused not by over confidence on the horse's part but, on the contrary, by *lack* of confidence, which means that somewhere along the line the rider has been at fault.

It is more than likely that the horse has been asked to do too much jumping too early in his training, and that he has been ridden at fences when he is out of balance and lacking impulsion. As a result, he finds the whole business of leaving the ground a bit scary and wants to get it over and done with as quickly as possible.

Cure

The first thing to do is to restore your horse's confidence. To do this you must encourage him to relax, at the same time building up his impulsion. As soon as your horse shows any signs of rushing, stop jumping over consecutive fences and revert instead to trotting poles, small grids and individual little jumps. He will only find jumping easy if he is going forward in the approach to a fence but always remember that going forward – impulsion – is not the same thing as going faster.

Trotting poles and grids will help to make the horse jump more calmly and in a more rounded outline and will enable you to keep him balanced and going forward from your leg. When he is coping with them in a controlled manner, start riding him over individual small fences. After jumping one fence, settle him down by circling him or even, if necessary, going back to a walk, before trying another one. If he shows the slightest sign of wanting to rush, keep circling in front of each fence and only ask him to jump it when you feel that he is calm and well balanced. Always keep the approach to each fence *short*.

It may take a long time to cure a horse who has developed a habit of rushing, but patience will eventually be rewarded. Once you have convinced a horse that jumping is not something to be frightened of, he should be happy to approach his fences calmly, going forward from your leg, but in a controlled, balanced way.

REFUSING AND RUNNING OUT

Horses stop at fences for a variety of reasons. They may be in pain, frightened or confused, bored with jumping the same old fences day after day or tired because of lack of fitness. Most refusals and run-outs are the result of rider error, not naughtiness or stubbornness on the part of the horse. Ideally the horse should never be put in a position where he wants to refuse, but mistakes are bound to happen now and again. When they do, it is important for the rider to work out what has gone wrong rather than simply become cross with the horse.

Cause: The horse is in pain
When a horse who is usually a good jumper suddenly starts to refuse, it is likely that he is suffering discomfort of some sort. Perhaps you have been unwise enough to ask him to jump on hard or rough ground. If so, he may have jarred his feet and/or legs. Discomfort in his mouth or back may also prompt a horse to start refusing.

Cure
Find out where he is hurting. Ask your farrier to examine the horse's feet. It there is no problem there, get your vet to check for leg or back problems. Make absolutely sure that your bit and bridle fit correctly and that there is nothing wrong with the horse's teeth or any part of his mouth. Check that your saddle fits correctly. However well it fits, don't forget to use a good numnah as well to help cushion the horse's back. Check that the girth is not pinching.

Cause: Lack of confidence
Poor riding and the horse's consequent lack of confidence in you are the chief causes of refusals and run-outs. Whether it is a question of asking a horse to jump something that is too advanced for his level of training, or not having him balanced in the approach to the

fence, the blame lies with the rider, not the horse.

Incorrect or insufficient flatwork results in the horse being unable to canter to a fence in rhythm, balanced and with impulsion, the three vital ingredients of successful jumping. Bringing the horse in to a fence too fast, without his hocks well under him, or 'hooking back' all the time, unbalances him. So does the habit employed by some riders of 'dropping the reins' in the last few strides to a fence and so losing all contact with the horse's mouth. Other riders seem incapable of steering a straight line towards a fence. All these mistakes make it easy for a horse to duck out to one side if he feels that it would be easier than jumping.

Another common mistake is to sit too far forward during the approach, thus putting too much weight on the horse's forehand and making it easier for him to stop when he gets to the fence, than to lift himself off the ground.

Overfacing a horse – asking him to jump something that he is not ready for or is simply not capable of jumping – is asking for trouble. So is a half-hearted approach on the rider's part. Horses are quick to realize if their riders are scared or lack determination.

Slippery ground conditions, causing a horse to slide as he is about to take off, will also undermine his confidence.

Cure

Go back to jumping very small fences and only increase the size when you are sure your horse has regained his confidence. Do lots of

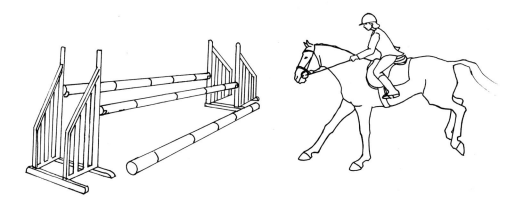

A small ascending spread with a good groundline gives the horse confidence.

flatwork to improve his rhythm, balance and impulsion. Practise over trotting poles and grids.

Keep a constant contact with his mouth throughout the approach to a fence and practise riding to your fences on a dead straight line. In competition it is normally only necessary to jump at an angle when you are competing against the clock. Check your position in the saddle – don't sit further forward than necessary or hurl yourself up the horse's neck at the moment of take-off.

Never ask a horse to jump something that is too much for him or, for that matter, for you. If you have doubts about your own ability to jump a particular obstacle, don't attempt it. Your horse will immediately sense your uncertainty or fear and, depending on his character, will either become frightened himself or will take advantage of your half-heartedness.

If a horse takes a dislike to a particular fence, it is probably because he was taken by surprise when he saw it for the first time. Always keep new, strange obstacles very small to begin with and remember that a wide fence with wings and a groundline is more inviting to a horse than an narrow 'airy' one. Let your horse follow another more experienced jumper over a fence that makes him spooky, to show him that there is nothing to be frightened of.

Always fit your horse with studs to suit the ground conditions. This is particularly important when jumping out of doors, where slippery ground can seriously scare a horse.

Cause: Too much jumping

When you are learning to jump it is natural to want to go on and on practising as you try out new fences and work on improving your style. This is fine if you have access to a stableful of horses but if you have only one mount, you can hardly blame him if he becomes fed up with jumping. Like human beings, horses are happier if they have variety in their lives.

Cure

Keep your jumping sessions short and vary your horse's work from day to day. Don't keep jumping him over the same few fences in the same part of your field or school. Changing things around will help to keep him interested. Always stop jumping while he is still enjoying himself. Don't ask him to jump every day and avoid the temptation of competing too often.

Cause: Lack of fitness

Jumping is quite strenuous work for a horse and he cannot be expected to perform well and enjoy himself if he is out of breath and has aching muscles. Show jumpers do not need to be as fit as, say, three-day event horses, who have to do a lot of galloping, but they must be in good physical condition. Make sure you build up fitness gradually.

Cure

Make sure your horse is getting enough energy-giving food for the amount of jumping you want him to do. You don't want him to be uncontrollable but he should be feeling fit and well. Give him plenty of regular work on the flat to help to keep his muscles toned up. Never overjump him: it is better to stop while he is still keen than force him to do one more round. Remember that tiredness leads to injury.

Cause: Disobedience

Now and again a horse will 'try it on' and refuse or run out simply because he is feeling in a naughty or stubborn mood. Much will depend on the individual horse's character. Indecisive riding by a previous owner may have convinced the horse that he can do as he likes with you, too.

Cure

If you are absolutely sure that there is nothing wrong, either with the horse and his training or with your riding, then you are entitled to reprimand him for refusing. You must, however, be very quick if you decide to give him a smack. He should still be facing the fence when you use your whip, not circling away from it. Worst of all is the rider who punishes a horse after leaving the arena. By that time he will have forgotten what he has done wrong and will, quite rightly, become resentful.

When you come in to a fence again after a refusal, you can give extra encouragement by using your voice and by slapping the horse down the shoulder once or twice with your whip to prevent a second stop. If you try to hit him behind the saddle, you will as likely as not throw him off balance as well as encourage him to run out to the side away from the whip. Watch racehorses in a finish and you will soon see how quickly and how far some horses swerve away from the whip.

Horses with a naughty or stubborn streak need strong riding. This is why you should always be careful to choose a partner who really suits your personality and riding talents.

JUMPING TO ONE SIDE

Cause

If your horse insists on jumping to the right or left instead of straight, it is probably the result of stiffness. Remember that horses, like humans, are born right- or left-handed. Pain in his back may also cause a horse to veer to one side when he jumps.

Cure

Have the horse's back checked. If there is nothing physically wrong with him, concentrate on suppling him equally on both sides. Make sure that your work on the flat includes lots of serpentines and circles on both reins. Jump small fences on a circle, too.

Resting a pole on the wing of a fence (one end in a cup, the other end on the ground) on the side to which the horse jumps will also help to keep him straight and prevent run-outs.

JUMPING FLAT

Cause

Riding to fences too fast or taking off too far back tends to make a horse jump with his back flat or hollow. In that shape he is more likely to hit a fence, especially with his hind legs, than if he jumps in a round outline.

Cure

As always, do plenty of corrective work on the flat. The horse cannot jump a fence in a round outline if he is allowed to canter with long, flat strides. The canter must be controlled, round and full of forward movement but not rushed.

Encourage the horse to round himself by working him over trotting poles and grids, keeping the distances short. To begin with, jump from trot, not canter, and put a placing pole on the ground in front of individual fences. Start with a distance that your particular horse finds easy then gradually

A horse that jumps with a flat back and a high head carriage makes more effort over a fence than one jumping in a round outline.

move the pole a bit closer to the fence so that he has to take off closer to it.

Jump him over plenty of small parallels, gradually making them wider. If you keep the approach slow and controlled he will have to 'use himself' to clear the spread, dropping his head, raising his shoulders and rounding himself while he is airborne.

RELUCTANCE TO ENTER THE RING WHEN COMPETING

Cause

By nature horses are herd animals and some are more unwilling than others to leave the herd – in this case the collecting ring. With a young horse it is probably just a case of strange surroundings making him nervous but if a horse becomes really nappy it may be because he remembers a previous bad experience in the ring and is totally out of love with competing.

Cure

Ideally, your horse should have been trained throughout his life to go away from other horses willingly when you ask him. It is all part of teaching him to be an obedient, pleasant ride. You can only increase his confidence in going off on his own by repeatedly asking him to do so under all sorts of circumstances, not just when you have to enter a jumping ring.

It is always a good idea with a young horse to take him to several shows *before* you ask him to compete just to let him get used to all the strange new sights and sounds. Walk him about, let him stand and watch the activities in the arena and don't be in a hurry to ask him to concentrate on jumping competitively. Only when he is relaxed and listening to you will he be in a position to do himself justice.

Leading a reluctant horse into the arena may help to give him confidence. BSJA rules permit an assistant, either mounted or on foot, to lead a competitor in provided they leave the arena the moment the competitor is inside.

A really nappy horse would probably need retraining professionally, but if his heart is obviously not in the sport he would really be far better off doing something else.

TRYING TO LEAVE THE RING

Cause

A horse who slows up and tries to leave the ring every time he passes the exit during a jumping round is again demonstrating his desire to be with the herd. Some horses are more prone to this than others but basically it is a question of poor training and poor riding. The surest way to develop the habit is for a rider to head for the exit immediately after jumping the final fence.

Cure

When you finish jumping a round

always do what you see the professionals doing: circle your horse to left or right so that he has to turn away from the collecting ring before you pull him up. With a horse who is just starting his jumping career, this should prevent him anticipating the finish and getting into bad habits.

If you are unfortunate enough to have acquired, unknowingly, a horse who is already inclined to try to leave the arena, it will take strong riding, probably with the aid of voice and whip, to cure him. If he is out of love with the jumping game, you will either have to stop jumping him for a while and concentrate on reschooling or find a more co-operative partner.

CHAPTER 7

GOING TO SHOWS

Amid all the excitement of setting off for a show, especially your first one, it is easy to overlook some important detail, so always plan for competitions well in advance.

Several days beforehand, make sure that your horse's shoes are in good order and that the screw holes for the studs have not been damaged. Clean them out and repack them with oiled cotton wool. If you have any doubts about the state of his shoes, consult the farrier at once – don't leave it until the day before the show when he may be too busy to help you.

If you are travelling to the show by trailer or box, check the day before that the interior is clean and ready for loading. If you are boxing your horse for the first time, practise loading him once or twice in the weeks before the show. It is essential to do this with a horse who has never travelled before and advisable even if you have been assured by his previous owner that he is easy to load. Even laid-back horses sometimes need a little time to get used to an unfamiliar vehicle. There is nothing more frustrating than being held up on the morning of a journey because you suddenly find that you cannot get your horse up the ramp first time.

Make a list of the equipment you will need for yourself and your horse and lay it out the night before so that on the morning of the show all you have to do is load it in the box. A last-minute search for some vital item will leave you in a state of nervousness before you even get to the competition!

CHOOSING A SHOW

So many shows are held throughout the year nowadays that wherever you live you should have little difficulty in finding something suitable. If you belong to a riding club, then you need look no further because all clubs organize competitions to suit their members and some have really excellent facilities. Many of the bigger riding schools run a regular programme of events, too. Pony Club members are also catered for with a wide range of competitive activities.

For a more comprehensive selection of show jumping fixtures, study the 'what's on' listings and advertisements in the various equestrian magazines. In the early spring, some of these publications produce special show numbers containing hundreds of show dates. These

Equipment Checklist
Prepare the following items the day before the show:

For the Horse

Rugs/roller
Leg bandages/Fibagee
Knee boots
Tail bandage/tail guard
Hock boots (optional)
Head guard (optional)
Headcollar and lead rope
Lead bridle and long lead rein

Saddle
Bridle
Martingale, if used
Breastplate, if used
Overreach boots
Tendon boots
Studs and tools for fitting
Spare girth, stirrup leathers and
    reins in case of breakages

Grooming kit
First aid kit for minor injuries
Feed
Haynet
Large water container
    (fill on morning of show – not
    all showgrounds have easily
    accessible taps)
Water bucket

For the Rider

Shirt
Tie or stock
Tiepin
Breeches or jodhpurs
Boots
Jacket
Hat with chin harness
Hairnet if you have long hair
Gloves
Whip
Spurs, if worn
Waterproof coat in case of bad
    weather

First aid kit

issues are useful to keep by you all year.

To begin with, it is not necessary to belong to the sport's governing organization (in Britain the British Show Jumping Association), although if you wish to take up jumping more seriously later on, you will need to become a member and to register your horse in order to jump in the wide range of classes run under official rules.

For the beginner, however, there are plenty of 'unaffiliated' shows and quite often BSJA-affiliated ones also run some competitions open to non-members riding unregistered horses. These are called 'minor' competitions, in which the prize money (in cash or kind) does not exceed a modest level, stipulated each year by the Association. The same rules also apply to 'local' competitions, which are open only to competitors living within a 24 km (15 mi) radius of the show.

The great thing at this stage is to choose the right class for you and your horse and not to be overambitious. It is better to compete for a while in classes that you find easy than to try something too difficult and give either your horse or yourself, or both, a fright.

Clear-round competitions are an ideal way of getting started. It is often possible to enter them on the actual day of the show, though be sure to check this in advance to avoid disappointment. The entry fee entitles the rider to attempt the course once. Usually, a rosette is awarded to each horse who goes clear. If time permits, you may be allowed to jump a second round on payment of an additional entry fee. There is no jump-off and therefore no pressure to go against the clock. A couple of rounds in this type of class is a good introduction to jumping in public.

If you belong to the BSJA and have registered your horse, you could make a start in the preliminary rounds of the Novice Championship or, if you have a horse who has already won a few hundred pounds, in the Newcomers. The BSJA rule book, issued annually to all members, gives full details of entry requirements for all its competitions and tells you exactly how big the fences will be and what can and cannot be included in a course (for example, novice horses and Newcomers are not required to tackle a water jump).

Make a habit of checking competition conditions carefully until you become familiar with them. That way you will avoid suddenly being faced with a type of obstacle that you have never practised over at home.

Having selected a show at which you would like to compete, write to the show secretary, whose name and address will be included in the show's advertisement, asking for a schedule and entry form. Don't forget to enclose a large, stamped, addressed envelope.

The schedule will list all the classes being held, with details of starting times, conditions of entry and, quite often, the approximate height of the fences as well. Choose the competition or competitions that suit you and your horse and complete your entry form *legibly*. Send it off with your entry fee to the show secretary, to arrive in good time before the final date for entries (this will be printed in the schedule).

Don't risk being disappointed by sending in your entry form at the last minute. Some shows do take late entries, but such an enormous number of people compete in novice competitions that in many cases shows have to limit the number of entries they can accept.

TRAVELLING

The first golden rule about going to a show is to allow yourself plenty of time to get there. Aim to arrive at least an hour before your class is scheduled to start – longer if you are unfamiliar with the show-ground, the parking arrangements, location of the secretary's office and so on. The worst thing when you are going to compete is to end up in a rush. If you are in a panic, you won't ride well and you will unsettle your horse.

Hock boots.

A Poll guard fitted to a headcollar.

He should be given his breakfast at least an hour and a half before your departure time. To protect him during the journey, he will need bandages on all four legs. Don't put them on too tightly otherwise they might restrict his circulation. The bandages should be put on over Fibagee or some other similar padding and should cover his limbs from just below the knee and hock to the coronet.

Knee boots, again not fitted too tightly, will protect his knees from bumps and, if he is inclined to fidget when travelling, it might be wise to fit hock boots as well. Some horses object to hock boots at first so don't put them on him for the first time on the morning of the show. Get him used to wearing them in the stable during the preceding weeks. If you find that knee and hock boots tend to chafe him, put a layer of cotton wool or some other padding under the top straps.

If you are unlucky enough to have a horse who is a bad traveller, it is a good idea to put overreach boots on him as well, just in case he jumps about and strikes into himself.

He should wear a tail guard over a tail bandage, again not put on too tightly, and a rug or sheet, depending on the weather, secured with a roller. A poll guard fitted to his headcollar will protect him should he throw his head up in the air and hit himself on the box.

Before being loaded, he should be dressed in all his travelling gear plus his headcollar, with a bridle over the top with a long lead rein attached. On the majority of occasions, most horses load perfectly well wearing just a headcollar with a lead rope, but if your horse does happen to play about unexpectedly, you will have far more control if he is wearing a bridle, too. It need not have a noseband and can be slipped off once he is in the box or trailer and your assistant has fastened the back strap or bar and put up the ramp.

Tie him up with his headcollar rope, not so short that he cannot move his head, but not so loosely that he can reach over and bite his travelling companion, if he has one. Remember that you should never tie the horse up until the rear fastening is in position. If he decides to run back he will probably break his headcollar and he could injure himself badly if he panics. Similarly, when unloading, always untie the horse and put on his bridle before the ramp is lowered and the rear bar or strap unfastened. Try to encourage him, by handling him calmly and talking to him quietly, to back out in a controlled manner, not in a mad scramble. Horses who rush back down the ramp can very easily hurt their legs.

Once all your equipment has been loaded and the horse has been boxed up, you are ready for the off. If you are travelling a long way or if the weather changes dramatically while you are on the road, be sure to stop now and again to check that the horse is comfortable. To prevent them losing condition, horses should be kept at an even temperature when travelling, so be prepared to remove a rug or add an extra one during the journey.

Whoever drives the box or the car pulling the trailer should take the greatest care to give the horse a smooth ride (another important reason for not setting out at the last minute and having to make a mad dash to the showground). Corners and roundabouts, particularly, should be taken slowly and carefully so that the horse is not thrown off balance.

If your horse is unused to travelling, try to take him out for a few short practice runs before going to a show for the first time. It will give him a chance to get used to this strange new sensation and once he knows there is nothing to be afraid of, he should relax and become a good traveller. Horses who become upset during travelling are often too tired by the time they arrive at the showground to perform well in the ring.

AT THE SHOW

Check your horse over when you arrive at the showground to make sure that he has not come to any harm during the journey. If all is well, you can leave him in the box while you go and find the secretary's tent. Or, if you have a competent helper, you can unload and let them take off the horse's travelling gear, tack him up and walk him about quietly to stretch his legs.

Collect your number from the secretary, confirm that you are in the right class and check the starting time. Your number should be

Loading Tips

To avoid problems when loading your horse (or if he is already difficult):

U Always allow yourself plenty of time and always have someone to help you.

U Position the trailer or box alongside a wall or hedge (it will act as a wing and prevent the horse from dodging out to that side).

U If possible, position the vehicle so that when the ramp is lowered it rests on higher ground than where the vehicle is standing. This will reduce the steepness of the ramp. Many horses dislike going up a steep ramp but will load quite happily if it is nearly level.

U If the vehicle has a front ramp as well, lower it (keep the front bar fastened) to let in as much light as possible. Horses don't like going into dark boxes. Put the light on if there is one and open any groom's doors as well to let in additional daylight.

U Have a haynet ready in the box to entice the horse in.

U Lead him to the box. He should be wearing a bridle over his headcollar and his protective travel gear. Walk by his shoulder and keep him straight as you approach the ramp. Don't get in front of him or try to pull him.

U If he walks straight in, have your helper fasten the rear strap immediately to prevent him going out backwards again.

U Tie him up, remove the bridle and let him eat his hay. If he has never travelled in this particular vehicle before, give him a feed, too, so that he has time to get used to his new surroundings. Do this a couple of times before taking him to a show. If he has never travelled at all, take him for a few short practice runs as well.

U With a nervous horse, try enticing him with a bowl of food in your hand, or load another, steadier horse first. Always handle the horse calmly. Don't rush him.

U If he refuses to go up the ramp or keeps jumping away from it, attach a lunge rein to one side of the back of the vehicle, pass it round behind the horse's hindquarters and ask your helper to hold it and put pressure on his quarters as you attempt to lead him in. If he still won't move, try lifting his feet one at a time and putting them further forward on the ramp. At the same time, your helper should keep the lunge rein taut. Both of you should wear gloves.

U With a very difficult horse, you will need two helpers. Attach a lunge line to each side of the box and cross them over behind his quarters, with a helper standing on each side and again exerting pressure with the lunge lines. Everyone should wear gloves to prevent rope burns in case a rein or lunge line is suddenly pulled through their hands.

U Remember that a horse who is difficult to load has probably had a bad time when travelling. Make sure that the stall is big enough for him. Horses usually find it easier to keep their balance if they can stand at an angle to the direction of travel. A horse who panics during transit can often be cured if the partition is removed, giving him more room to spread his legs.

attached securely to your arm or waist so that the number is clearly visible to the judges.

Next find the collecting ring. At big shows there is a draw for the order of jumping but at small ones riders can usually decide when they want to go by writing their names on a board provided for the purpose and positioned in or beside the collecting ring. If you can, put your name at least halfway down so that you will have a chance to see some of the other riders jumping the course before your turn.

A plan of the course will usually be put on display in the collecting ring about half an hour before the start of the class. Study it carefully. Note the position of the start and finish, the number and type of fences, the direction in which they must be jumped, the rules under which the class is being judged and the time allowed. Memorise the course and make sure that you understand the rules. If in doubt, ask someone to explain. The stewards are there to help. If it is a jump-off class, note which fences will be included in the jump-off course just in case you go clear.

Tack up your horse, not forgetting his boots, and fit studs in his shoes in plenty of time.

WARMING-UP

The amount of warming-up you do will depend very much on your particular horse. In theory, he will need the same amount of riding-in before he goes into the ring that you give him at home when schooling. In practice, though, things often turn out differently at shows. Some horses become very excited by the buzzy atmosphere of a showground and require much more work before they will settle down. Only experience will tell you how long to allow under competition conditions. If it is any consolation, top international riders don't always get it right either!

At your first show, try working your horse at a steady trot, and then in canter, on straight lines and circles for about ten minutes. If he settles down quickly and is listening to your aids, let him relax until shortly before you are due in the ring and then give him a few practice jumps over the fence or fences provided in the collecting ring.

Base what you do on how he behaves at home. If he usually requires a lot of work before he will concentrate, allow yourself more time. If he is a relaxed individual, just do enough to loosen him up. The important thing is not to tire him out before the competition. There is no need to keep jumping him over and over again, either. By this stage you should both know how to jump. All you have to do before competing is to ensure that your horse is supple and obedient.

During his time at the show, try to let him rest as much as possible so that he conserves his energy for the actual competition. Once you have ridden him, dismount and loosen his girth. If it is a hot day, keep him in the shade; if it is cold, keep him well rugged up.

A typical course plan for a jumping competition. Make sure you study the plan before you walk the course.

WALKING THE COURSE

Shortly before your class you will be allowed into the arena to walk the course. Be there in good time and take full advantage of this opportunity to inspect the fences at close quarters. By all means go in the company of a more experienced rider who will give you valuable advice but don't waste time gossiping with your friends.

Walking the course in the correct order of the fences will help fix the route in your memory. Plan how you will approach each fence and where you will begin to make your turns. Measure the distances in any combinations and try to work out how they will suit your particular horse's stride.

Note if there are any particularly spooky things alongside the arena – flags, or a bandstand or something else that your horse might not have seen before. If there are, make a mental note to ride him past there when you first come into the ring so that he is less likely to spook when he is actually jumping. Be absolutely sure that you know where the start and finish markers are. You will be eliminated if you miss one.

After you have walked the course, stand and watch the first few riders jumping it until it is time to get mounted. This will give you the chance to see how particular fences are riding and where the main problems are. Be in the collecting ring in good time, ready to go into the arena as soon as you are called by the steward.

RIDING THE COURSE

Trot quietly into the ring when your number is called and, once inside, go into canter and circle round until you hear the start bell. If you are sent in while the previous horse is still jumping, walk quietly along the side of the arena until he has finished so that you don't distract him.

Don't forget to take the opportunity to canter past any potential ringside distractions to give the horse a chance to get over his surprise before he starts to jump.

Listen for the bell. After it rings, you have thirty seconds (the time stipulated under BSJA rules) in which to prepare and go through the start. Aim to approach every fence straight and dead centre and be prepared to do half-halts between fences to keep your horse's quarters well under him. Keep him going in a nice rhythmic canter and take care to ride the turns correctly so that he does not fall out of balance. If he knocks a fence down, don't panic. Forget about that one and concentrate on jumping the next one better.

If he has a refusal, circle round and ensure that you get a good balanced approach for a second try. If he knocks into the fence as he refuses, the bell will ring and you will have to wait while it is rebuilt. Go back to where you intend to start your new approach and circle him round until the bell is rung again to say that you can go on. If you have three refusals, you will be eliminated, the bell will ring and you must leave the arena.

Remember that the excitement of being at a show may affect both you and your horse. Don't lose your temper or become flustered if something goes wrong. If your horse refuses or knocks a pole down, the chances are that you have not ridden him at the fence correctly, or perhaps it was something he had not seen before and he was simply taken by surprise. If you become angry under these circumstances, he will come to think of jumping in public as an unpleasant experience and may not be so willing to try next time.

When you have jumped the last fence, go through the finish and then circle round, still in canter, before pulling up and heading for the exit on a loose rein.

If, for any reason, you decide to retire before completing your round, indicate your intentions to the judge by pulling your horse up and raising your hand.

THE JUMP-OFF

If you go clear and it is a class with a jump-off, you should stay in or near the collecting ring until your turn comes to go again. Unless you were one of the last to go in the first round, there will be time to dismount and give your horse a breather until it is time for the jump-off. Loosen his girth and walk him about to cool him off and keep him supple. If it is cold, be sure to cover him with a rug. Remount shortly before your next turn. You can give him another little jump over a practice fence if you have had a long wait but he won't need much warming-up having already jumped a round.

Remember that jumping against the clock calls for a lot of skill on the part of both horse and rider. It is not simply a question of a mad gallop round the course. Competitions are usually won by horses who can turn quickly and jump accurately from a short approach. These skills take a good deal of practice so don't expect to win first time out. Ride sensibly and concentrate on keeping your horse balanced and going in a nice rhythm. It is better at this stage to complete another steady clear round and collect a rosette for a placing than to go all out to beat the clock and make mistakes in the process.

Horses that are often asked to jump at speed may well get into the habit of jumping flat.

AFTER THE COMPETITION

After finishing the competition, loosen your girth and walk your horse around to cool him off. Take him back to the box, untack him and rug him up. Offer him a drink and some food. Whenever possible try to stick to a horse's normal feed times. If you are going to be at the show all day, he will need his usual lunch and a haynet. Of course, he must not be fed immediately before work, so if the time of the class clashes with his feed time, he will have to have his food later than usual.

He can stand in the box for a while if you want to stay on to watch some of the show, but don't leave him cooped up for too long, getting bored and tired. If you are not competing again, put his travelling gear back on, box him up, give him a haynet and take him home to the comfort of his own stable at a reasonable hour.

CHAPTER 8

GENERAL CARE OF THE SHOW JUMPER

All horses and ponies benefit from a regular routine of exercise and feeding. Like their owners, if they live in a happy, comfortable environment, they are more likely to be happy and contented themselves and to enjoy their work. Looking after the show jumper, like caring for other competition horses and ponies, takes time, skill and a certain amount of money. You can't leave him standing in a field all week and then expect him to come out and win prizes at a show on Saturday.

He needs to be fit without being uncontrollable, and well fed without being fat. Feeding and exercise go hand in hand. They are the two most important factors in getting and keeping a competition horse fit for the work expected of him. It must always be remembered that, like human beings, horses are individuals: some tend to stay as thin as greyhounds no matter how much they eat, others will put on weight on the most meagre diet. Some are greedy, others have to be tempted to eat. There are lazy horses, energetic ones, overexcitable ones and laid-back ones.

The art of the good trainer is to study each individual horse or pony

and to work out a suitable diet and exercise programme for his particular needs. If you are an inexperienced horse owner, take time to learn about the various types of horse feed and don't be afraid to ask for help from a knowledgeable person (such as your instructor) in planning your horse's daily work routine and feed.

FEEDING

As with all horses and ponies, the basic rules of feeding the show jumper are:

- Feed little and often – three or four times a day is best.
- Feed only good quality food.
- Feed at the same times each day (but make adjustments as necessary on show days).
- Make fresh water freely available (when this is not possible, always offer water *before* a feed, never afterwards, which could cause colic).
- Never work a horse immediately after feeding – he needs at least an hour to digest a small feed, longer to digest a bigger one.
- Don't leave unwanted food in his manger.
- Never make sudden changes, either to the quantity or type of feed.

Total quantities, divided between bulk (usually hay) and hard food or concentrates (oats, cubes, coarse mixes, barley, maize and so on) will vary according to the individual. As a very general guide only, a big pony (14 h.h. and over) needs around 7.3–9.5 kg (16–21 lb) of food daily, while a 16 h.h. horse will consume around 12.7 kg (28 lb). Again as a general guide, for horses and ponies in work about two-thirds of the daily intake should be bulk feed and about one-third concentrates.

Good quality hay is vital for competition horses. Because dust (a term used in a general sense to include the fungal spores that occur in both hay and straw) can seriously affect a horse's lungs and, in turn, his performance, many people now soak their hay in water at least overnight, and sometimes for up to 24 hours, before feeding. A useful alternative is HorseHage, grass that has been cut (but not dried like hay) and then sealed in bags. It has the advantage of being dust-free. Because it is richer than hay, it must be fed in smaller quantities.

Hay is very often fed in a haynet which must be tied quite high on the wall to prevent a horse getting his foot caught in it. This tends to result in less wastage than if it is fed on the ground, but there are two very good reasons for not using a haynet. First, it is natural for a horse to eat at ground level. This is, after all, what he does when grazing. Second, a horse's training is designed to lower, rather than raise his head carriage. The stabled horse spends many hours a day nibbling at his hay and to allow him to do so with his head stuck up in the air does not seem totally logical! Many show jumping riders prefer to feed their horses from chest-level or low-level mangers, which prevent too much wastage but ensure that the horse keeps his head and neck in a more natural position when eating.

The type of concentrates you give your horse will depend on the type of individual he is. Show jumpers don't need the same quantity of oats as, say, racehorses, who are required to gallop at top speed. In fact, many horses can be made fit enough for jumping without any oats at all. If you find your horse becoming too excitable for comfort, try reducing his oat ration or cutting it out altogether and substituting specially formulated competition-horse nuts or cubes.

Don't forget to check with your supplier that the feed you are giving your horse is free from 'forbidden substances'. These include all sorts of drugs and other substances which could either mask an injury or illness or improve a horse's performance. They are listed in the rule book of the sport's governing body and since spot checks are made at many shows, it is up to the rider to make sure that he has not, even inadvertently, given them to his horse just before a competition. (The same warning applies to veterinary treatment. If your horse has to be given medication, check with the vet when the substance will have cleared the horse's system and when he can, as a result, legally return to competition.)

FITNESS

Getting a horse or pony fit to go show jumping is much the same as getting one fit for any other form of riding. When he first comes up from grass he must be given walking exercise only, to build up his muscles. If you ask him to do faster work or jump too soon, you may well cause strains and sprains.

As a rough guide, you should start with about three-quarters of an hour's walking a day and gradually increase this, over a period of two to three weeks, to an hour and a half or two hours a day. Never allow the horse simply to slop along. By keeping him going forward in a steady rhythm and keeping him straight, you will start to build up muscle in the right places. It helps to keep his interest if you can vary the routes you take each day. Give him a day off once a week, to relax.

During weeks three–four he can begin trotting, at first for short periods only, and always at a controlled, rhythmic pace. Always walk for at least ten minutes before starting trot work, to limber him up and again afterwards, to cool him down. Too much trotting on the roads can cause jarring, so never trot flat out and try to trot uphill rather than on the flat where possible, as this helps to reduce the jar on the horse's legs.

Two or three sessions of flatwork can be introduced during the fourth week. Keep them short – no more than about 20 minutes – and work mostly at walk and trot with only a little cantering. Take him for a quiet hack afterwards.

There is no finer way of building up muscle and improving the capacity of a horse's lungs and heart than hillwork. Horses who are turned out on hills invariably come in fitter than those who live in flat paddocks, and a weekly session of hillwork will keep a competition horse fit just as effectively as a lot of fast canter work, with far less strain on his legs. During week five of your fitness programme, introduce one session of hillwork if you can. Continue with regular hacking and flatwork and start doing a little work over grids.

By the start of the sixth week, your horse should be looking and feeling much fitter and he can be given a canter work-out. Let him stride on, without going into a flat-out gallop. Cantering uphill is the most beneficial but, above all, only canter on good ground. Hard, uneven ground or very muddy conditions can so easily cause tendon, foot or muscle injuries.

After his six-week fittening programme, your horse should be ready for more serious work. To prepare him for competition you will need to concentrate on his flatwork and do some jumping practice, starting with grids and then going on to single fences and small courses. To prevent him becoming stale, don't jump him too often – two or three times a week is plenty – and alternate his schooling sessions with

Stabling and Grazing

Ideally, you will have your show jumper stabled at home where you, or a member of your family, can attend to his daily needs and generally keep an eye on him. If you have no facilities of your own, the alternative is to keep him at livery. This means stabling him in rented accommodation, which, for convenience, should be as close as possible to home.

Full livery, where you pay the owner of the yard for the complete care of your horse, is a good option for the first-time horse-owner, who will need plenty of expert advice, or for someone with very limited time. If it is a well-set-up yard, you will also have the benefit of being able to use their jumping equipment in a proper schooling arena.

Part livery, where you pay for basic services only and do much of the work, such as grooming and exercising, yourself, is cheaper and means that you will spend more time getting to know your horse or pony.

Wherever you keep your show jumper, he will need a draught-free, roomy loose-box, preferably situated where he can see other horses or at least some form of

human activity to prevent him becoming bored. Turning him out to grass for part of each day (when the weather is suitable) will help him to relax but be sure that the field is securely fenced. It is not unknown for horses to jump out of their fields once they know how!

As a precaution, always fit boots or bandages when you turn him out, to guard against injury. Most horses like to have a bit of a buck and a gallop when they first go out and it is all too easy for them to strike into themselves or jar their legs. For the same reason, make sure that your field is free of rubble and the fence has no projecting bits of wood, metal or wire on which he could injure himself.

Although it is nice for horses to have other equine company, it is usually safer not to turn them out in groups but to put them alone, or with just one 'pal', in adjacent small paddocks, so that they can see and talk to each other but not get close enough to argue and possibly injure one another by kicking.

Limit the amount of grazing time you give your horse if he is inclined to put on weight quickly and the grass is rich.

---

hacks out in the countryside, some hillwork and the occasional fast canter to clear his wind. Hacking should be enjoyable but it should also be used for continuing your horse's education and improving your riding skills. Make sure that you keep him moving forward, in balance and with a good outline.

During your horse's fitness programme, introduce him to hard

feed very gradually to prevent the digestive problems that can accompany a sudden change from a diet of grass. Start with one small daily feed during the first ten days or so and then increase it to two. In week four he can be given three small feeds a day and by the end of the six weeks he can be on his full working ration, preferably divided into four small feeds.

Don't forget to fit his legs with protective boots during all your exercise sessions.

BEDDING

Your horse will need a deep, comfortable bed to encourage him to lie down and rest, to keep him warm and to protect him from draughts and knocks. Straw makes a particularly comfortable bed, is economical to use because it is easy to muck out and is relatively easy to dispose of.

However, some horses are allergic to the dust in straw and others tend to eat it, which is bad for their wind. It is also difficult to stop greedy horses, who need to be kept on a strict diet, from becoming overfat if they insist on eating their bed. Wood shavings and shredded paper make good alternatives, although paper is not easy to dispose of and will probably have to be burnt.

GROOMING

A thorough daily grooming or 'strapping' with a body brush, followed by a wisp, helps to keep the horse's muscles toned up, as well as keeping his coat clean. Before exercise, it is sufficient to give him a quick grooming, to remove straw marks and any dirty patches, and to pick out his feet. However, you should allow up to three-quarters of an hour later in the day to strap him, clean his head, brush his

mane and tail thoroughly and cleanse his eyes, nose and dock.

Unless you are going to a show, your main grooming should take place after he has finished work. If he has been clipped, or if the weather is particularly cold, don't remove his rugs completely – fold them back while you are working on his front half and forward while you groom his quarters.

On show days allow yourself plenty of time to give him a good grooming and to plait his mane before you load him in the box. Then all you will have to do when you get to the show is to add a few finishing touches, such as oiling his feet, spongeing his nose and tidying up his tail. Groom him again when you get home, to remove any sweat or mud.

CLIPPING AND TRIMMING

If you plan to do indoor jumping during the winter months, then your horse will need to be clipped to avoid excessive sweating and subsequent loss of condition. A horse who grows a very thick winter coat will need clipping right out, including his legs (leave a saddle patch to protect his back). A thinner-coated horse can be hunter, blanket or trace clipped. Some horses may need to be partially clipped during a hot summer, too.

Always have your horse neatly turned out for shows, with his heels trimmed and his mane and tail pulled. A nicely pulled mane need not be plaited for shows, though an unruly one will look better plaited than left loose.

SHOEING

Regular shoeing – about once a month – by a good farrier is essential for the show jumper, who can so easily be injured by a loose shoe or a risen clench. Screw holes for studs are required on all four shoes. Never use studs in worn-down shoes: the stud may be longer than the depth of the shoe and could injure the hoof. When a horse comes back into light work after a holiday, his first set of shoes can be fitted with road studs. These cannot be removed and when he starts serious work he will need new shoes with screw holes for jumping studs.

RUGS

Stable rugs may be made of wool-lined jute or a range of modern manmade fabrics. The latter are usually much lighter than the old type of jute rug and are often fitted with a clever arrangement of cross-over surcingles which makes a roller unnecessary. Where a roller is used, the anti-cast type (with a metal loop over the top) is the best. It must be well padded and fitted over a foam pad to reduce pressure on the horse's back. Whatever you use, the important factors are that the rugs keep the horse warm and that they fit correctly. Any undue pressure on his back or girth area

Health Care

All horses need to be vaccinated against tetanus and then given regular boosters. Vaccination against flu is also widely used nowadays. In fact, it has been made compulsory by the organizers of some equestrian events and you should make sure that your horse has a vaccination certificate and that he is given boosters at the correct intervals, otherwise he may not be allowed on certain showgrounds.

Worming is another vital part of your horse's health. If he is kept stabled, he needs worming when he comes in from grass and again when he goes out but if he spends time in his paddock each day he will need worming every six to eight weeks.

Because jumping is such a strenuous type of activity, horses can suffer all types of strains and injuries. However careful you are about not jumping a horse until he is really fit, not overjumping him and protecting his limbs with boots and bandages, the show jumper's legs, feet and back are always going to be at risk. Never delay sending for the vet if your horse shows signs of being lame or otherwise unwell. A horse who suddenly loses his enthusiasm for jumping is probably hurting somewhere and needs expert attention and, more than likely, rest.

could cause a sore patch and prevent you jumping him for a while.

If your budget permits, a smart day rug for use at shows is a nice addition to your equipment, otherwise your horse can travel in his stable rug.

A waterproof rug is a great bonus to have on hand at shows, to protect your saddle and keep your horse warm. When he goes out to grass he will need a New Zealand rug. On cold days, particularly if he is clipped, the horse will probably need an exercise sheet to keep his loins warm while you are working him. Use a fillet string, which goes under his tail, to keep the sheet in place.

STABLE BANDAGES

Bandaging the horse's legs when he is stabled helps to keep him warm and prevent injury. Stable bandages should always be fitted over padding and never put on tightly since they are not designed to support the leg, merely to protect it.

CHAPTER 9

RIDING A SHOW JUMPING COURSE

To the casual observer, one show jumping course probably looks much like another. There are, after all, only a limited number of types of obstacle and someone with no knowledge of the sport probably imagines that it is simply a question of scattering them around the ring and waiting to see which horse can jump the highest.

In reality, it is far more technical than that. Course designers don't have to resort to making fences bigger and bigger in order to find a winner. As has already been discussed, something as seemingly simple as the positioning of a groundline can dramatically affect the difficulty of a fence. A good course designer also has many other problems with which he can test the ability and level of training of the horse and the competence of the rider without asking them to jump enormous fences.

These include double and treble combinations, related distances between individual fences, and obstacles of unusual design. Really difficult technical problems will only be used at the top level of the sport, but even relatively novice competitors need to know more than how to jump over simple individual fences.

Safety Checklist

Always have someone with you when you do jumping practice, in case of accidents.

Always wear a crash hat with the chin strap fastened.

Always wear riding boots or shoes with a heel, never trainers or Wellingtons.

Check your tack regularly, particularly the stitching, and have it repaired immediately if any part of it shows signs of wear.

Never jump on hard, rough or very muddy ground.

Always fit your horse with protective boots when jumping.

Fit studs when jumping out of doors.

Use strongly made fences for practising, not flimsy bits of wood or rusty oil drums.

Only build practice jumps that will fall down if the horse hits them.

When using guide poles, rest them in cups on the wings, not on the top pole of the fence.

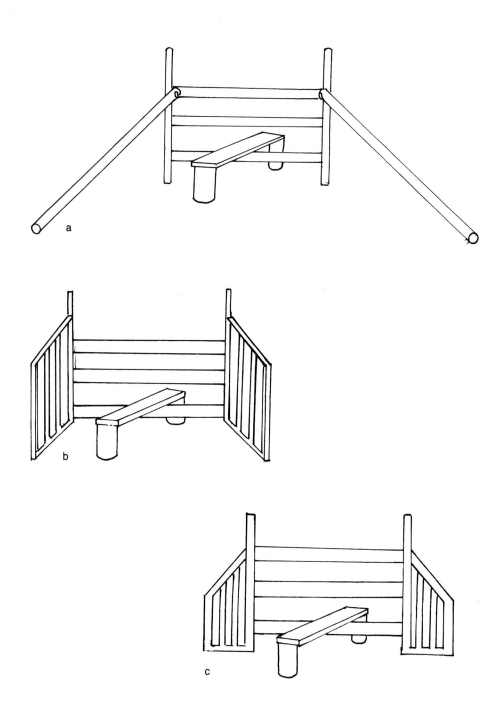

Narrow fences are more difficult to jump than wide ones. (a) Guide poles make the horse's job easier; (b) angled wings also help; (c) straight wings also present a more difficult problem.

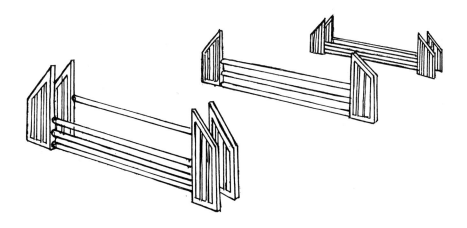

A treble combination comprising ascending spread, upright and parallel: the easiest type for the novice.

NARROW FENCES

A fence such as a stile or narrow gate is sometimes included in a course as a test of accuracy. Narrow fences are much more difficult to jump well than wide, inviting ones. They tend to look much less imposing and the horse is more inclined to be distracted and to misjudge his take-off point. Some horses may decide it is easier to go round small obstacles rather than to attempt to jump them.

An accurate approach to a narrow fence is therefore crucial. Your horse must be well balanced and full of impulsion and, above all, absolutely *straight*. Practise jumping narrow fences at home – a set of rails or a wall no wider than 1.8 m (6 ft) will do.

Anything that funnels the horse towards the fence will make it easier to jump. To start with, try using a guiding pole on each side. Rest one end of each pole on the ground and the other in a cup on the wing. When you can keep your horse dead straight and jump the fence bang in the middle every time, practise jumping it without the guide poles but with the wings placed at an angle. In the end you should be able to jump the fence successfully with the wings straight and no guide poles to help the horse.

TREBLE COMBINATIONS

Except in competitions for the very inexperienced horse or pony, you will soon find yourself having to jump simple treble combinations as well as doubles.

A treble can be built of three

upright fences, three spreads or, more usually, a mixture of the two. The easiest fence going into a combination is an ascending spread. This is an inviting fence and should ensure that the horse jumps in a good outline and does not land too steeply. An upright fence going in is the most difficult as it might make him 'back off' and land so steeply that he finds the distance to the next fence too long. This is difficult enough in a double, but in a treble a mistake at the first fence will affect the way he jumps the second *and* third fences.

Keep things easy when practising at home. Use the 'true' distances already described on page 58 for simple doubles. Start with two strides between each fence to give you and the horse more time to sort things out if you make a mistake. Then reduce one of the distances to one stride. A good combination for an inexperienced horse and rider is an ascending spread followed by one stride to an upright and then two strides to a parallel. Keep the fences small.

room for the rider to make an adjustment to his approach to the second obstacle.

Always measure related distances when walking the course (you will find more related distances between fences at indoor shows because of the lack of space). Your aim should be to put in as many strides as the course designer intended but you must also be prepared to make adjustments if your horse has an exceptionally long stride, an exceptionally short one or if he lands too short or too far out over the first of the two related fences.

Watching other riders over the course may be helpful but remember only you can choose the best way of going for your horse.

If you do get the first fence wrong, you will need to use one or more half-halts to build up the horse's impulsion immediately after landing so that you will then be in a position to ask him to lengthen or shorten his stride as necessary. Try to make your adjustments as soon as possible after landing, not just before take-off at the next fence.

RELATED DISTANCES

A distance of three, four or five non-jumping strides between two fences is known as a related distance. This is because the way a horse jumps the first fence, and how far out he lands, will have a direct bearing on his approach to the next fence. If there are more than five non-jumping strides between two fences, there is usually

When practising over related distances at home, use the following measurements:

U three non-jumping strides 14–14.6 m (46–48 ft)

U four non-jumping strides 17.3–18.3 m (57–60 ft)

U five non-jumping strides 20.7–21.9 m (68–72 ft)

DITCHES AND WATER JUMPS

By nature most horses are suspicious of holes in the ground and also of water but since the show jumper will at some time have to tackle both, it is sensible to prepare yourself well in advance. If your horse has been hunting, or done other cross-country work, he will be less worried by the sight of water and ditches than if he has only ever jumped over coloured poles. When out hacking take the opportunity to pop him over the odd ditch (providing the take-off and landing are safe).

Ideally, you should find somewhere with a selection of permanent ditches and water obstacles over which to practise. However, if that is impossible, it is not too difficult to construct at least a water ditch at home. It needs to be only a few inches deep and a few feet wide. The base can be made of concrete and painted blue to resemble the water jumps used at shows. The most difficult part is to get the base absolutely level so that the water does not drain away.

The water ditch can be incorporated into a variety of little fences, starting with a low rail over the top. Make it as inviting as possible for the horse by using wings and guide rails. If your horse has never seen water before, let him have a look at it before you ask him to jump it and get a more experienced horse to give him a lead a few times. He must be kept balanced and full of impulsion during the approach and you should be prepared for him to hesitate at first and then put in an ungainly jump.

It is a good idea to dig a dry ditch as well. Old railway sleepers staked into the ground can be used to support the sides and, again, the ditch can be incorporated in upright fences, ascending spreads and parallels.

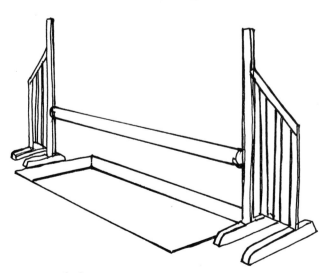

A small fence over a water ditch.

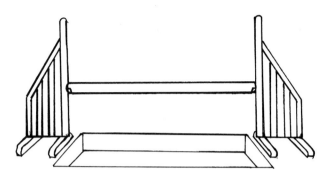

A small fence over a dry ditch.

The advantage of having your own permanent ditches and water jumps is that you can pop your horse over them every time you have a jumping session. In the end, most horses will get over their nervousness and jump a fence built over a ditch as confidently as if the ditch wasn't there.

A water ditch can also be used as a first introduction to jumping wider water jumps. Simply place a sloping brush fence or sloping board, about 60 cm (2 ft) high, in front of the ditch and a slightly higher rail over it and you have a small water jump.

If you have access to a wider water jump or can have one constructed at home, so much the better. It need not be wider than about 2.4 m (8 ft) because you can

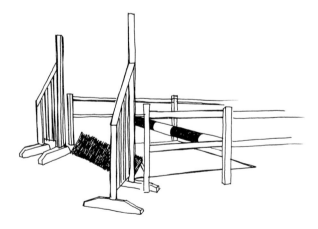

A waterjump with sloping brush fence and a rail over the water. The angled wings help guide the horse to the fence.

always increase it by pulling back the fence on the take-off side. Remember that it is essential for the landing side to be safe. It should be sloped and covered with rubber matting to prevent jarring if the horse lands short. As with the ditches, make the jump look inviting by putting angled wings on either side, and place a pole over the water to encourage the horse to jump upwards as well as outwards.

To clear a wide water jump, the horse will need a bit more pace than usual but there is no need to approach at a gallop. Too much lengthening of his stride will simply make the horse jump flat, whereas to clear width he needs to gain a fair amount of height, too. Concentrate on having the horse balanced and full of impulsion and on getting him to take off as close as possible to the sloping brush or board. In competition, he won't incur faults if he knocks this provided that he doesn't put his feet in the water.

The getaway from a water jump is as important as the approach. Often a course designer will follow the water with an upright fence, which will only be jumped successfully if the horse is well balanced and can quickly get back into a rhythmic stride.

JUMPING AGAINST THE CLOCK

There are several ways of saving time in a jump-off. Making tight turns is the most energy-saving for

Dos and Don'ts
♡ Do remember that jumping is not a natural activity for a horse or pony so…
♡ Don't expect him to be perfect.
♡ Do give him lots of encouragement and praise him when he does well.
♡ Don't lose your temper with him, it was almost certainly your fault.
♡ Do remember that all riding is potentially dangerous, so take sensible safety precautions.
♡ Don't be in too much of a hurry – get the basics right first.
♡ Do behave sportingly at shows, win or lose.
♡ Don't forget that horses and ponies are not machines – they need holidays too.
♡ And finally…keep a sense of humour and enjoy yourself. Show jumping is supposed to be fun!

the horse and all your work on the flat, designed to make him supple, obedient, well balanced and full of impulsion, will help here. Where the course allows for it, you can also save time by increasing speed between fences. This is where the horse's ability to lengthen his stride without falling out of balance comes into play. Novice horses, however, should never be raced round jump-off courses. It simply encourages them to flatten, lose impulsion, make mistakes and frighten themselves.

If the course is not too big, you can sometimes save valuable seconds by jumping the odd fence at an angle. To practise, build a small parallel with a good ground-line and begin by trotting to it, with the angle of approach not too acute. Then practise at canter, on both reins, and increase the angle slightly. Don't overdo the angle, otherwise you might encourage the horse to run out.

A well-schooled horse will also be able to turn in the air over a fence, another means of landing facing in the direction you want to go. You can indicate your intentions to your horse while you are still in the air by putting more weight in the stirrup on the side to which you want to turn and also opening your hand on that side, away from the withers, to turn his head.

INDEX

Page numbers in *italics* refer to an illustration